# Magog:

# The Blessed People

By

Stanley E. Wachtstetter

## Prologue

Upon arriving in Russia in late 1915, Andrew Bar David Urshan discovered to his utter dismay that his passport has been stolen. En route from his native Iran, he had planned on spending the night in St Petersburg but now his itinerary had been foundered. Russia at this time was reeling from the storm of the Bolshevik Revolution, and Andrew was a frightened and stranded traveler who likely would become a target for the roving mercenary soldiers hired by the authorities to execute any suspicious persons or dissidents.

He located a boarding house and met people who seemed friendly enough. This boarding house would become his lodging for a short time until he could rethink his next move. As was his custom, whenever he connected with open hearted people, he began ministering the Word of God to them. One evening while speaking to a small group a loud noise disrupted the service. Standing in the doorway was a wild-eyed soldier brandishing a rifle. The soldier, speaking loudly in Russian, demanded to know who the speaker was. The man who oversaw the establishment explained the situation to the soldier who then instantly ordered the other soldiers into the room. Andrew Urshan could see that a firing squad was being organized. Urshan is now 30 years old and from his youth had prayed earnestly to God and possessed a great devotion to his Savior. He had decided that if he ever faced death, he would die worshipping and praising God. The lead soldier walked Andrew to the wall of the room and pressed him prone against it. The Officer crossed to where his soldiers were and aligned them into a firing formation as the few people watching huddled together in terror. The head man ordered his men to raise their rifles and take aim. Urshan knows death is eminent and lifts his hands to God as the officer raised his arm to signal firing. Words of prayer tumble from Andrew's lips when suddenly with shock wave intensity, he starts speaking in an unfamiliar language. The utterance continues for several minutes as time seems to stop, and when he opens his eyes he discovers that the room is empty save those in attendance at the meeting who are hovering in a corner. Andrew asks the lady interpreter what happened, she answers with a question, "Where did you learned to speak such articulate Russian?" Andrew states he knows none of the Russian language, she then explains that he spoke with such authority to the soldiers that, "if you pull your triggers, the giant men behind you will kill you instantly, "she then indicated to Andrew that the soldiers must have seen the large ones because they ran screaming into the night.

This divine intervention of biblical proportions would open the door for the apostolic message across Eurasia for the next 100 years and more. To date upwards of 1,000,000 people have encountered their Pentecost and the Jesus Name message in Russia. Stan Wachtstetter and UPCI missionaries as well as other Oneness Apostolic groups have continued the powerful legacy of Andrew David Urshan with great success. Thank you, Stan Wachtstetter, for giving us an amazing front row seat into one of the most historic works of God in modern times
Nathaniel Paul Urshan

# Foreword

This book was developed for the teaching session at a Bible School in the Old Soviet Union at the Living Water Church at Izmial, Ukraine over the Christmas holidays of the centennial of the baptism of A. D. Urshan.

The year 2016 was the centennial of the baptism of A. D. Urshan, and his founding of the Christian Evangelical Church in the Spirit of the Apostles. This was a good year to be teaching on the history of these things.

Sadly, the people of this region have been robbed of a beautiful and rich heritage which is theirs. They began civilization and from this geographical point it spread throughout the world.

It is my hope that this book will help build a bridge of better understanding between those in the West and those in the East and especially among the Oneness Pentecostals.

This is an expansion of all I have written, including Nathaniel Urshan and my work in Russia. I want to thank Norman Rutzen for taking interest in what I am doing and sending me both pictures and writing at length his memories of those events. I wrote all I had been able to glean around and about the event of their meetings in Moscow; however, when I received his account I decided to include it with almost no editing. Bishop Rutzen's account is of great value by being a primary source. It is a firsthand account.

I want to thank Mike Robertson who has been such a blessing in my life. He provided me with funds and a place to be able to sit and write. He took me on a "Five Star" tour of the Holy Land. There, Janet Trout showed us around and, especially, Scythopolis. I learned how Bishop Trout had loved running up the Tel at Beit She' an/Scythopolis. She has been involved with tourism there for many years and is a great person to make arrangements. She took me all over Scythopolis in a golf cart.

I wish to thank our Soviet brothers for preserving their history, which they shared from both their oral tradition and written documents. After all these years to have documents from that time giving firsthand accounts is amazing.

Those who helped the making of this book possible with pictures, contributions, time and energy:

N. P. Urshan

Norman Rutzen

Samuel Smith

James N. Larson

Mark Dean

Paul Mooney

Mary and Greg Harris

Helen Wachtstetter

Mike Robertson

Table of Contents

# Chapter One

## In the Beginning

If we take the Biblical description, in the book of Genesis, to find the geographical spot where Eden was located, we will see the description of two Rivers that are easily identified, and two over which Bible scholars will argue. Locating the Tigris and Euphrates is very simple as it flows across the entire region of Mesopotamia north and south. Note that the headwaters are up in the country of Turkey and come very close to touching or do touch the Black Sea. Another River, Pison, in which the Bible says, "there is much gold there" has an even better description in more modern translations which refers to "er aromatic resin". The region just north of the Black Sea was extremely rich in gold, and in fact, to a very large degree, identifies the people of that region. To this day, the resin of amber is seen to be the identifying rock or mineral of Russia. This seems to be a likely area for Pison.

Generally, the Garden of Eden is placed to the south of Turkey and the Black Sea which is close enough that it still would be identifiable with the people of Ukraine, Russia, Georgia, Armenia and other countries in this region. I would postulate, placing the garden just a little farther north and placing it in the bottom of the Black Sea. We need not quibble over this point, but I find it of interest.

I want to emphasize the importance of the Black Sea and the entire region. This body of water will serve as a microcosm for the entire world. On the east will be the western part of Asia, and on the west, will be Europe. To the south will be the Middle East, including Turkey, Iran and Iraq. To the north will be the land of Japheth of modern-day Russia and the mainland of Europe. It is said that this great sea is a drainage of a huge deluge.

Scientists attributed this runoff to the melting of a glacier after some ice age, but I like to think of it as the run off from that great flood. After all these years, it is still draining. It has springs at the bottom and was once a fresh lake, but today there is a small opening connecting the sea with the Mediterranean and from it out into the North Atlantic and part of the ocean system.

If God wanted to start a new world there is no place better suited to do that than at this spot. To the north is cold, to the south is hot. You have here the balance of man to whatever might best suit him. You can rapidly see Europeans living to the north and spreading out across the countryside. And to the south the Asiatic and the descendants of Ham spreading across the Middle East and down into Africa.

In this book, we will keep coming back to this region like a child returning home to its mother. People from this region will live in Israel and be there at the time of Jesus. Andrew and Peter will travel to this region to do their missions work. Revivals will spread across this country side. Andrew David Urshan will be born in this region and minister in this region.

The seven churches of Asia will be just to the south of the Black Sea. Nathaniel Urshan will travel here, and I will have the opportunity to make over seventy missionary trips into this region. We will use this as an orientation point north and south of this body of water.

It would seem that God had some special love and providential plan for this region. After the spread of men and his failure we will come to Noah. Traditionally there is a mountain in Turkey with the name of Ararat, and generally this is viewed as the place where Noah landed. However, the Scripture says, "the mountains of Ararat." Just as there is a mountain called Ararat, there was also a region or kingdom called Ararat and referred to as Urartu. This land and this kingdom pushed up to the Caucasus Mountains and thus they could be termed - -the Mountains of Ararat. It is my opinion that Noah's Ark landed in the Caucasus region. My view of this fits the Scripture but is based more on archaeology and anthropology. There is a thing called the Kurgan Hypothesis in which he finds the spread of all proto – Indo –European (PIE) man coming out of this region to spread out across the world. At first this idea was built on the systematic spread of the wheel and the horse. In more modern times this has been established by DNA.

The horse is of interest because it originates from the Americas but is wiped out and suddenly reappears in this region. From here it spreads across Europe and is brought back to America. This is consistent with the Bible account of the ark. Archaeologists will note the spread of men by keeping track of the spread of the horse. I keep emphasizing this place is the likelihood of Noah's landing as the dominant spread of man is from the north and the horse and the wheel will be absent to the south in Sumer and Babylon.

This is consistent with the Scripture that gives reference to the fact that "as they journeyed from the east" which gives the idea for a group of people in constant motion and yet in chapter nine of Genesis it seems that Noah has settled down in this spot attending his vines. The vast group remains mobile and traveling. Now in a sense Noah and his son Japheth are proto -Scythians. This is reinforcing linguistically by a teaching that was common in the Soviet Union called the Japhetic Theory. The theory shows a linkage between common words in Russia and that of the Middle East in the populating of a common origin.

Let us use the Black Sea as the center of all activity. It would be here in the sea or shortly to the south we would find the Garden of Eden and on the Black Sea to the northeast or the southeast would be where Noah landed. From here mankind begins to spread forth.

There is close to the Black Sea on the north, stretching out eastward, the city of Maykop. Close to this city is a kurgan or a burial mound and from this we have gathered a great deal of information about the early people of that region. It would be consistent with the Biblical account of Noah. Even in the city of Izmial, Ukraine (where I visited so often), I noticed great vines of large size everywhere. The horse which is indigenous to the Americas will be wiped out and will mysteriously and suddenly be domesticated and dominant in this region. Maykop Culture will become the early culture and will be significant.

The Scythians which will be the key people of this region and can be viewed as similar to the Native Americans, will be tribal with many family tribes and one tribe after another leaving this area and going forth to settle other cultures in other regions. There will remain some identifying characteristics that make it clear that they came forth from the original family. One of the main characteristics of all the early Scythians will be the fact that they did not like to build permanent homes or towns. Of course, there would be those that would settle down and build homes, but most of the people were in motion. To this day one of the battle plans used by Russia over and over goes back to their ancient mobility. The idea of continuing to draw their enemy further and further into the country without a direct battle until they are so far in that they cannot escape.

The Scythians lived on their horses and they had wagons on wheels, and as such they were constantly moving. Thus, there were some that had wooden structures and houses in which to live, but the majority were in motion. Think of the gypsies and you have an idea of their lifestyle. The Biblical phrase "as they journey" is very appropriate for these people as they would've been constantly in motion.

Darius came up against this when he tried to invade the land. Darius had been successful conquering most of the world but when he came to the Scythians he found them constantly moving and staying out of reach but always close enough that he knew they were just out of reach. In frustration, he complained and asked them to stop. The commander of the Scythians sent him this answer, "If I fly before thee, prince of Persians, it is not because we fear thee. What I do now is no more than what I am used to doing in the time of peace. We Scythians have neither cities nor lands to defend; if thou wouldst force us to engage thee, come attack the tombs of our fathers, and then thou shalt find what manner of men we are." He continued to chase the Scythians until they had drawn him to a point where he could not escape.

The Scythian chief then sent a messenger with a bird, a mouse, a frog and five arrows. He told him something like "unless you can fly like a bird, or go to ground like a mouse, or swim like a frog, you will not avoid our arrows". You might find it of interest that the word Scythian means "arrow" or "archer".

Now all that brings us to Maykop and let me explain why I believe this is where Noah settled with Japheth and his children. First are the grapes of which the Bible is very specific that Noah began to cultivate. Archaeologists agree that grapes were first domesticated in the area north of The Caucuses and between the Black Sea and the Caspian Sea. This happens to coincide with the Maykop region where the oldest terraces in the world are found. This grows out of the development of grapes and the tending of them. Noah in this work was far bigger than anything most of us can imagine. Remember all civilization had been wiped out right down to the ground. It simply said he was a gardener of vines. Our mind immediately flashes to grapes but let us think of other vines. The dove in returning to the ark had brought with it an olive branch. This was prophecy and inspiration that God pointed him in a direction. Remember, olives are a vine that grows into a tree. The apple tree, as is strawberry, blackberry, plums and a few others are all the rose family, which is a vine. Maykop means a "valley of apple trees."

The Maykop Culture will be highly developed in a way consistent with the Scythians, identified with gold, and a likely place where Noah had settled with Japheth and his sons Gomer and Magog. Enter now an incident with Ham, the eldest son, that seems to have been demoted while Japheth becomes the favorite because he had honored his father. I see this in Japheth naming his eldest son Gomer, which according to Judaism means "stand for the family."

There is great speculation of the Biblical account of what exactly happened with Noah and Ham, but I think the Bible is very clear, and it centers on disrespect for his father. Japheth took the lead and showed sensitivity and respect for Noah. This seems to have endeared Japheth to Noah and moved him to be listed first among the generation.

I am speculating, as I love to do, that Noah lived with Japheth, Gomer and Magog and so on. Can you see Magog sitting on Noah's knees and him telling little Magog about the ark? At first, they would likely live on the ark, but God landing them on the mountains would force them down and out of the snow and cold.

Noah and the Indo-Europeans would become Magog or Scythians. By the time of the Greeks they would describe these people with the physical characteristics described in a variety of sources as a group with red hair and blue gray eyes which I still see in Russia often these days. One of the dominant tribes that will come out of here will go north. Some to Scandinavia and some to Germany, and according to the Jewish concept of the spread of men will form Gomer which will settle in Germany. This group will also be called the Celtic people or Saxons, and these will settle later in Scotland, England and later the great melting pot of the Americas. Those in the Scandinavian regions will later return to Mother Russia as the Rus. There is a detailed listing of the nations from Noah in the Judaica Encyclopedia.

The Black Sea will be the home of the early part of the book of Genesis and will be the place where Adam and Noah will live. Their exact precise location will either be north or south of this lake. Here the Scythians will dwell and spread forth nation after nation - -Parthians, Medes, Hittites and one after another across the whole of Europe and the Middle East and Asia. As the Roman Empire grows it will incorporate most of this region, especially to the south of the Black Sea. Names will change and some of the region will be known as Macedonia and some as Thrace, but always with the idea of the Scythians in the background.

The Scythian empire will stretch across the steppes of the Ukraine and lower Russia. Under various names the Scythians will have a highly-developed culture. The fact that they favored riding horses continually and having wagons in which to live, does not minimize the culture. They were a fierce fighting group that was feared throughout the civilized world. They will dominate Russia and Ukraine for centuries and later be copied by the Tartars, which will control this region until about 1000 AD. Josephus writes that the Scythians were those the Jews called Magog.

The Scythians were famous as fighters and as horsemen. They were also skilled with the bow and arrow and as such, warriors will one way or another be recruited to fill the Roman army. They went all over the world as Roman mercenaries. There were so many and did such a good job that seemingly The Roman Empire gave them a city in what is today the nation of Israel. Israel at the time of Jesus had ten Gentile cities most of which were "beyond Jordan." The most interesting city was one with an incredibly long history the Jewish people call Beit She' an, but was called Scythopolis in the time of Christ. This was an ancient city going back before Abraham and was the administrative center for the Egyptian empire for the region. It was for many centuries a very famous Jewish City, but the Romans remodeled it into a glorious city and apparently gave it as a place for Scythians to retire. It was the largest of the Decapolis, meaning ten cities, and served as its capital and was the only one of the two cities on the west bank of the Jordan. Jesus preached through the Decapolis and as such must have gone through this beautiful city. This is always my reminder that Jesus preached to the Russians.

Jesus loved all people and was constantly reaching out. Even though he came to his own and his primary ministry was to Israel, he was always reaching out.

Tartarstan Mosque, Greg Harris praying for Russia.

## The Book of Acts and The Time of the Apostles

We will now begin to reflect on the early history of the church in apostolic times and the interaction of the church and with the Scythians/Magog. Let us consider Jesus sending the witness out into the world. Those at Pentecost, and the apostles going into the region that would later be the Soviet Union. Here is my emphasis to underline and highlight the region of the Black Sea, the Scyths and the area that was later the Soviet Union.

The purest history of the Apostolic Church is found in this historical book of the New Testament—The Acts of the Apostles. The Book of Acts is a two-volume set with the first volume being the Gospel of Luke. Acts the first chapter and the first verse makes it clear that he is writing to an individual named Theophilus. This seems to be a Roman official, possibly governmental. It may also be poetry of a fictitious nature, as the name means "Lover of God," and as such he may be addressing this to all people that love the Lord.

These books of the Gospel of Luke and the Acts of the Apostles - -sometimes called the Acts of the Apostles Peter and Paul - -are good history and detailed geography. The work is likely done jointly with two great scholars Luke and Paul. Luke was a doctor and Paul was highly trained in theology. It is also of interest that Paul was born in Tarsus in what is today Turkey. At least we are certain he was a Roman citizen of the city. Paul has his citizenship from this region but may never have lived there. It may be that he grew up in Turkey and went to Israel later, or was from a wealthy family that had holdings in Turkey but lived in Israel? The point being, here we return to the region of the Black Sea with this connection of Tarsus. He was Jewish, but a Roman citizen. Luke is a Roman name. This is a turning point of the gospel becoming primarily gentile. Some say the two books are written to show how the gospel went from Jerusalem to eventually the city of Rome and their region in the Middle East. From Israel became a gentile church strong in the Roman Empire. With two great scholars that were cosmopolitan and adapted to travel across the Roman Empire, the book is written late, obviously after the Gospel of Luke and most of the other gospels as there is no mention of the destruction of Jerusalem and thus it must have been written around 70 A D.

Acts the first chapter will open with Jesus and the disciples on the Mount of Olives; this would be close to Gethsemane, which means "Olive Press." On this mountain Jesus had prayed for Jerusalem and His people. It is here that He tells them to go on for the Holy Ghost. This hill is located about ½ mile from the Temple Mount.

Acts the second chapter is the setting that is Jewish, it is the day of Pentecost and they are in the center of Jerusalem. Pentecost is one of three Jewish holidays that every Jew is expected to take his family to Jerusalem. However, we will see God taking this event and turning it into a missionary out reach. Jews and converts will gather from all over the world. At the tower of Babel language was confused causing division, but at this Pentecost the Holy Ghost will cause people to speak in other tongues and this will be to unite. Now for a lesson here what is important is that the first language listed is Parthian. The Parthian Empire was just south of the Caucuses Mountains and was settled by Scythians. Other countries listed are Media, Cappadocia, Pontus and nations south of the Caucuses between the Black Sea and the Caspian Sea all pushing up into Russia. All these Jews would have gone on to tell their nation's testimonies of what they had seen and heard, especially those that were baptized that day or shortly after this date. This would carry the gospel including baptism in Jesus name and the infilling of the Holy Ghost up into the region of the Black Sea. Armenia will be the first nation to declare itself a Christian nation. The entire region will become receptive to the gospel and from here spread north.

The Black Sea was called the Inhospitable Sea, in part because of the peoples surrounding this Sea. But with the civilizing of the region and the building of Greek colonies across the southern side of the Black Sea and later, Roman colonies building all around the sea long before the time of Jesus and the apostles, the name had been changed to the Hospitable Sea. Now a very welcoming and lovely spot. Parthian, Medes, Cappadocians and people from all around this region will hear the Pentecostal message and carry it home to their synagogues. As in other parts of the world, congregations will develop, and they will want to share the message. With one colony after another surrounding the Sea, and all within walking distance the message will spread rapidly.

Peter will give the keynote message at Jerusalem on Pentecost, and the crowd will ask what they need to do. This will be a defining moment in which Peter will make it clear that they need to repent of their sins, be immersed in water with the name of Jesus spoken over them, and that they would receive a gift of the Holy Ghost. Peter made it clear that this was for all people and for all times. Beyond that the writer of this book said, "They continued steadfastly in the apostle's doctrine". This is important for those of us today that wish to be Apostolic and continue in the apostle's doctrine.

Let us consider five ways in which baptism or Acts 2: 38 has been changed by man-made doctrines. First, notice that what took place at Pentecost was spontaneous. There was no catechism or time of testing but immediately they were baptized, and the same manner immediately they repented. Second, they are immersed in water and no other way. Third, it was with the name of Jesus called over them. Fourth, it was with the full expectation that they might receive a pneumatic experience of receiving The Holy Ghost. Fifth that this was presented to them as a means of salvation and not just a ceremony of entering the church. You will notice that this will remain a consistent pattern throughout the Book of Acts, and throughout the letters to the churches. This was clearly the pattern for the first 100 years of the church with no Scripture indicating it would change during the church age.

We will see in the third chapter the name of Jesus used not only in baptism but in healing. It makes it clear that the greatest thing we were given in the church is his name and the use of his name. It is better than silver and gold. In Acts chapter four we will see them beaten for using the name of Jesus. They will be asked by what power or by what name did you do this. Can you imagine a man healed and able to walk and they are beating them and asking them by what name? This becomes one of the greatest scriptures of the Bible, "that by the name of Jesus Christ. . . Neither is there salvation in any other, for there is none other name under heaven given among men whereby you must be saved," Acts 4:12

Acts the eighth chapter will continue the history as the gospel now goes out from Jerusalem and is carried to Samaria. For this to take place the intervening chapters will introduce to us a new office in the church of deacon, to men such as Stephen and Phillip. We will read of growth in the church and the persecution will scatter the church. We will learn of Saul and his involvement. Phillip will carry the gospel to Samaria and we will see that it remains consistent in message and practice with Jerusalem and Pentecost. He goes down to Samaria which is geographically north of Jerusalem, but it is always said going down from Jerusalem. At this time, they had not been filled with the Holy Ghost. A very good question to ask is how did they know they had not received the Holy Ghost? Also, note that it is very clear they were baptized in Jesus name. There was concern shown that they had not received the Holy Ghost. Peter lays his hands on them and prayed for them to receive the Holy Ghost

Acts the 10th chapter is an earth shaking and reassessment of the church. It is extremely frightening to all men involved, and as a declaration that God had declared the gentiles equal with the Jews. It was God opening the door to the gentiles. For this to take place, God would use angels and visions and miracles and men such as Peter to make it happen. Again, note the consistency in apostolic doctrine and practice with that of Pentecost and Samaria. The Holy Ghost is poured out and they know it is true, "for they heard them speak with other tongues". Peter commanded them to be baptized in the name of the Lord Jesus.

Acts the 15th chapter is a gathering of the church and Apostles to once again consider the core message of the church. It was not for kosher laws of the Old Testament, but it was the message of Pentecost. They will reaffirm that God gave them the Holy Ghost. James in making his decision and note that it is James as the head of the church not Peter, quotes Amos the ninth chapter which was a prophecy concerning God and rebuilding the tabernacle of David and the gentiles being added to the church. The method of this taking place would be by having the name of Jesus spoken over them. James makes it clear that this was God's plan from the beginning of the world.

With a clear message that the door was open to the gentiles as they had received Cornelius and the council had decided that no burden will be laid on the gentile church, we will now start reading of the Apostle Paul's missionary travels. You will have missionary trips stretching out across Europe and some of them very close to this region. We will make special note of Acts the 19th chapter as it will reinforce again the significance of the name. It is estimated that this passage is decades after Pentecost and the church and its missionary activity has pushed out all over the world. The churches changed, and its nature remain Jewish to primarily gentile, but Acts 19 makes it clear that the core message of the church and its practices remain the same. Remember this is Paul and not Peter, and he is at Ephesus in what is today Turkey and not in Jerusalem. Paul comes across believers. Note they are believers and the Apostle Paul joins himself to them. Noticing something in their message seems to be off, Paul asks if they have received the Holy Ghost. The next question he asked was how they were baptized, and he explains they need to be baptized in the name of Jesus. Then he prayed for them and they received the Holy Ghost and spoke in tongues when they received it.

This event in the city of Ephesus brings us back once again to the beloved Black Sea region. He passed "through the upper coasts". This would have put him close to Bulgaria and the Black Sea.

This history gives us the four missionary journeys of the Apostle Paul; it will be massive and detailed showing the spread of the gospel throughout the world. We will come to the end of the book without the usual ending of "amen". It will just cut off because the gospel is still going out. The questions will have been answered, "How did the gospel get to Rome?" "How did it become a gentile church?" The last chapter will show the Apostle Paul trying to convert Jewish leaders and finally realizing God has blinded them. He says that God has turned to the gentiles because they will receive the Word. The Apostle Paul will remain two years openly teaching the Word of God. Was he released?

The biological brothers and apostles, Peter and Andrew went to the region of the Black Sea. There's no direct statement for this fact but abundance of circumstantial evidence. These brothers seemed to have traveled East together, but it is uncertain how closely they worked and traveled together in that region.

The Greeks did not call it Black Sea, but rather termed it the Inhospitable Sea because of the wild peoples living around the shore. Later they changed the name to Hospitable Sea once they had built colonies and domesticated the areas. It would have been a well-ordered world of Pax Romana that Peter and Andrew would enter. The Greeks had ordered it and then the Romans had built colonies. In fact, it would have been a resort area much as today. It was so nice that soon Constantine would move the center of power and the Palace to this region. The Imperial resort would be Niceae.

There is no Biblical, nor historical evidence nor reference indicating Peter ever visited Rome. In 1 Peter, he mentions the saints in Babylon sending greetings which could mean he was in the East in the literal region of Babylon or metaphorically referring to Rome? Now couple this with the first verse of that book and the countries mentioned: Pontus, Galatia, Cappadocia, Asia and Bithynia. Every well-ordered Roman province mentioned in this passage is just south of the Black Sea pushing up into Russia.

A couple important points: first, the Catholic Encyclopedia says it would be doubtful that Peter would write these without having visited them. Second, often people will argue Peter was just writing the Diaspora of Jews in general, but there is no mention of the main colonies Alexandrea or Rome. He only writes to those on the south of the Black Sea. This all seems to indicate Peter spent at least some time in the East preaching in the region of the Black Sea. How long he ministered there or if he spent the rest of his life there is unclear.

Andrew, being Peter's brother, would have found it natural to have traveled with him and ministered together. Later Andrew, with or without Peter, used the Black Sea and the Dnieper River to evangelize Magog (Scythians). Eusebius, the church historian, quotes Origin stating that Andrew preached among the Scythians. An ancient chronicle of the Kyevian Rus states that Andrew preached up the Dnieper River all the way to Kiev and then hiked over into what is now Russia. There are many other references, enough to establish his ministries in these areas. Andrew in tradition is designated the Patron Saint of Russia, and they will all say it was Andrew that brought Christianity to this area. For those that love the adventure of missions, one's mind can race thinking of the river, nature, the villages, and hungry souls. There were likely Jewish Synagogues, colonies of Romans, the organized Roman Province of Thrace, with villages peaceful and others wild. He would meet believers, some from Pentecost, others that had been evangelized, and still others that had never heard about Jesus.

Ships, ships, ships. The waterways and the seas will provide relatively easy travel. Remember, Peter and Andrew were fishermen and used to ships. Traveling around the edge of the Black Sea would be easy. It is today, and always has been, a world class resort area. Once on the Black Sea you can take the Dnieper River or some other river into the interior. The Dnieper is like our Mississippi River. It runs north and south dividing the country of the Ukraine. Also, at what is today Odessa, and was likely the same name at that time, runs the Danube River. All these waterways provided great opportunity for Apostolic missions.

I can tell from personal experience that where one goes many others follow. I am introducing a new way of viewing this region. Many, as Americans, have never considered the tremendous work of God taking place in this region at that time. Think of the hundreds in Apostolic times going across these regions sharing the Good News. These Scythians (Magogians) were our brothers, the church of God. As Paul wrote concerning the church, "Where there is neither Greek nor Jew, circumcision nor uncircumcision, Barbarian, Scythian, bond nor free: but Christ is all, and in all."

# The Seven Churches of Asia

## And

## Nicaea

The book of Revelation is generally thought of as prophecy and not history, but prophecy is simply history before it happens. The Seven Churches of Asia as found in the book of Revelation chapters two and three are seen by many to be an outline of church and social history. The seven churches are in present-day Turkey, between the Black Sea and the Mediterranean. This brings us back to the Black Sea region.

**Ephesus**: The first-time period, or church is Ephesus and refers to the end of the time of the Apostles. People had been living for God many decades now and holding to the apostolic truths but were losing their fire. They no longer longed-for revival or being in church. The love of Jesus was still there but no longer was the enthusiasm. God blessed them, and they were settling to enjoying the blessings of God.

Think of the drop in Apostolic doctrine and practice in such a short time period. In fact, the church will start becoming popular. Armenia will be the first church to declare itself a Christian nation. This early church in Armenia and all over the region will have many of the characteristics of the early church but be missing some and then be replaced with formal liturgy. The love is dying out.

They will replace love with works. They will slightly and slowly replace the desire for the return of the Lord with the church doing humanitarian works.

The Seven Churches of Asia will be laid out in a pattern reminding one of the Candle Sticks in the Tabernacle. It will be a U shape, lighting the whole world.

Ephesus was in present day Turkey about 250 miles south of the Black Sea and in the far west on the Aegean Sea. From the Scripture we learn the primary worship was love—Diana. This book is dealing with the historical projection of the church and society. We will start with a pure church that is free and dedicated to God and apostolic doctrine and practice, and then we will see society and the church join forces and dominate man and then God bring the church and society back to freedom.

**Smyrna** begins around 150 A.D. And is dealing with the heavy persecution of the church. God notices the faithful suffering and poverty. The root word is myrrh and is a beautiful fragrance when it is crushed. God has no condemnation, nor does he demand anything of this church. This period is a time of desperation. Everyone is doing what they can to live for God. North of Ephesus it is on the coast of the Aegean Sea and is closer to the Black Sea. The root word is "my".

**Pergamum** will carry us through the third century, which is a time of heavy persecution and martyrdom, and even closer to the Black Sea. In about 112 AD Pliny will write the Emperor Trajan and explain that he has sorted out a new religion that appeared to be Jewish but was in fact very different and called Christian. He explained how he persecuted these Christians. The Emperor wrote back complementing what he was doing but told him not to go out of his way to locate Christians. We can see phrases such as "the synagogue of Satan" and "those that say they are Jews and are not." The constant reference to martyrs speaks of this time, men such as Origin wanted to be martyrs so badly that his mother hid his clothes so that he could not go out. At some point, it degenerated into the worship of martyrs and saints.

**Thyatira** which was given to have interpreted the word to be throne and altar or a crown and a place of worship. At any rate this will be the introduction of the state church in the fourth century. It will be during this time that an Emperor of Rome by the name of Constantine will accept Christianity. In the West and among Protestants or Bible believing Christians he will be seen as a great evil. In the East he will be seen as the 13th apostle. He was likely, a very brilliant politician much like our Ronald Reagan. The comparisons between Reagan and Constantine would be monumental. Constantine was going to bring about a very great evil and the downward progression of society and the church, but it was an unintended consequence and I doubt that he had any intention of doing evil. He was clearly a Christian, a strong Christian, and he will be baptized close to his death and was, likely, baptized in Jesus name.

Constantine will unify the Roman Empire and move the center of power from the city of Rome to a new city close to the Black Sea and close to the Mediterranean that he will name after himself, Constantinople. Here in the West, we think of Rome as the center of power in the old world, when in fact it had moved east.

Constantine will accept Christianity and become its champion and Helena will go to Israel and build magnificent cathedrals celebrating the various aspects of the life of Jesus. He will call a council at Nicaea and invite 1800 Bishops to this convocation. He will pay for all their travel, give them each a Bible as a gift, which cost over a year salary, and provide them with free house and food. They each are permitted to bring two assistants with them, and three deacons to care for the Bishops. It is amazing that barely over 300 accepted the invitation. Of those that attended only five were from the West, and as most were from areas close to Niceae it is likely that there would be Bishops from north of the Black Sea, Thrace, Macedonia and others in the area of the Soviet Union. It is very likely; they were opposed to state involvement and did not trust the emperor. It was a glorious invitation of luxury with the Emperor serving the Bishops directly; it is remarkable so few accepted.

A creed was adopted at this council and today most people believe it to be as sacred as Scripture in that it was universally accepted, and many believe it has something to do with the doctrine of the Trinity. Most believe the doctrine of the Trinity originated here, and that the creed was universally accepted and was a Trinitarian statement. History is not so kind to their imaginations.

Let us keep in mind that the church existed for almost four centuries without these creeds or statements. Further, this council had nothing to do with the Trinity as it is what theologians call a Christological Council. The primary reason the council was called was that a bishop by the name of Arius had begun to teach, at Alexandria, that Jesus was not God.

Even though only a little over 300 Bishops responded to that call for this meeting it was still massive with each of them having an assistant, and three deacons. Constantine walked into the room dressed in purple and gold and invited the Bishops to be seated before he sat down. You can imagine after all the years of persecution and hardship, to now be treated so well. It must've been incredibly moving. No longer shutout, but now brought into the center of power. It was a changing time for the church.

The discussions and the arguments went on for days; Constantine did not attend but sent notes that cautioned men such as Athanasius who were arguing in a manner that most of the Bishops could not understand. Even after the creed is written only 220 of the 318 accept it.

I want to make it clear that in my opinion there is absolutely nothing, not one word, wrong with the creed adopted in 325AD. The issue of great concern is the state involvement. If the state can say their religion is correct, then it has the power to say the same religion is wrong. Freedom of religion is the most fundamental freedom because it is absolute freedom of thought and a freedom you share with God alone.  Here is the wording of the Creed of Nicaea.

The Creed of Nicaea

We believe in One God,

The Father Almighty,

Maker of all things visible and invisible;

And in one Lord, Jesus Christ,

The Son of God,

Begotten of the Father, the only begotten

That is, from the substance of the Father,

God from God,

Light from Light,

True God from true God,

Begotten not made,

Of one substance with the Father,

Through whom all things came into being,

Things in heaven and things on the earth,

Who because of us men and because of our salvation came down,

And became incarnate,

And became man,

And suffered,

And rose again on the third day,

And ascended to the heavens,

And will come again to judge the living and the dead,

Whose kingdom shall have no end...

The creed is similar to the statement the Apostle Paul makes at the beginning of every epistle in which he says, "Greetings from God the Father, and the Lord Jesus Christ." The word might better be translated even. Greetings from God the Father, even the Lord Jesus Christ. This is called the dichotomy and refers to the humanity and deity of Jesus, that he is God and man. But you must remember what was being discussed at this council. If people read it in the manner they interpret it with the Father and the Son but being separate entities, then Arius would have won the argument. That is exactly his position that the Father was God and Jesus was the lord or some great one.

At this council, like the Bible and the Apostle Paul, they are saying that there is within Jesus, God and man. But he was in fact a real man, but that he was also God. Whatever was said about God in the first paragraph was exactly the same God in the paragraph about the Lord Jesus. He is God of God.

The creed is Biblical and found in the Bible apart from the Greek word homoousios which means the same substance. Arius wanted to say that the Father and the Son were homoiousia or similar. It would be like taking two chairs from the dining room table that both looked alike and he was saying they are very much the same and they are almost the same. But the Bishops said that it was the same chair.

Now if, Constantine is a good man and if the creed is correct then what is wrong with this council? What is wrong is the involvement of the government in the church. This will begin a downward progression of men that will end up in serfdom and slavery. It will be the King and the Pope exercising absolute authority over people. This will continue until the peasant revolt and their radical reformation.

The second great evil of this council will be while it is all Biblical, but another council will be called 40 years later at Constantinople, which is today Istanbul and again so very close to where we have been writing about, and at this council many words will be changed and the meaning from a Biblical statement to a more manmade doctrine, and it will be the beginning of Trinitarianism. To confuse matters even more they will call this new creed by the same name - - the Nicaean Creed. They're trying to play on the fact that the first creed was so good. Bishops argued against the new statements saying this was not what they had agreed to. Remember the reasoning that if they can control your faith then they can change it any time they please, and you must submit to it.

**Sardis**: The next church or age in Revelation is the church of Sardis, and it is the absolute dead, cold, church of the Dark Ages. Back at Nicaea, they not only adopted a creed but began to spell out rules and regulations on the church. One of my favorite ones was that on Sundays they were not to kneel and pray but they were commanded to stand and pray. It was a very small thing, but the absolute beginning of control over men's lives through the State Church system and man was controlled body and soul.

**Philadelphia**: The next church is Philadelphia, or the church of brotherly love, and it will be the start of our revolution that will bring about freedom in both the church and society. If you love your brother, you will not want to control or dominate him. It will spark a revival that will produce the Reformation and more importantly an extreme separatist group calling for the separation of church and state and democratic ideals. Bible believers will seek a personal relation with God and the opportunity of salvation for all.

**Laodicea** is the end time church.

Russian Church

# Chapter Two

## Snippets of Spiritual Revivals Across Russian History

The general view of Russia is that it has always been such a tightly controlled society that nothing other than the approved church ever functioned there, and when alternatives were developed they were immediately stamped out. Now, to some degree this is true, but we might say it was more controlled in image than in reality. There were significant religious revivals that spread from time to time, that were identifiable, had leaders, and were significant enough that we can read about them and identify them. There were periods in their history that had less control than others, and during these times evangelical fervor might be very open. In addition, the lack of evidence of a solid Apostolic Church, teaching the One God, Jesus Name, Holy Ghost and holiness message does not equate with it not existing. What can be demonstrated is that all the elements that make up this apostolic fervor were present, and therefore, were likely that they existed together with all these other elements. It is true, that great effort was taken to stamp out the history of these people and to minimize their influence.

We have already seen that the apostles were ministering in this area, especially Andrew. Before 1000 A.D. there would have been a lack of written history across this whole region. During this time the Tartars had control of this region, and they together with other pagan forces likely made life difficult for believers. Tartars, in general, were not interested in interfering with the locals' religion or daily life, but they were not Christian, and later would be Muslim. There was a large Jewish community that had developed in these regions, and it would be difficult to imagine Jewish people fleeing here without Christians having done the same. Therefore, we can think of the history of evangelicalism in Russia in two major times with first being from the time of the apostles until 1000 A.D. and the second time being from 1000 A.D. till the present. This is because from 1000 A.D. the Russian Orthodox Church was developed and had a stranglehold over Russia during this time. Therefore, definitive groups can be clearly seen as they are opposed and declared heresies. Before this time, there would no doubt have been Christians and churches, but they would simply be recognized as Christians and not clearly defined. It would be our view that those churches started by Peter and Andrew would be by definition Apostolic and teaching the same doctrine found in Acts of the Apostles. There may have been Orthodox missionaries starting churches, but most would simply be Christian. Because of the persecution, they would need the Spirit and would have clung to truth or given up on all faith.

We can reason their existence because of the massive influx of Judaism over this time. That is to say, we know the Jews trying to escape persecution would flee across the rivers into the Ukraine and into Eastern Europe. They would be looking for someplace to survive with eventually there being large communities of Jews. Because the Romans had a hard time separating between Christians and Jews in the very earliest days and because there was still persecution of Bible believing Christians after Constantine accepted

Christianity, we can reason that in the same manner they also would escape to this region.

## Stringolinki

In the 1300s there developed a group of Stringolinki the origin of the name is lost in history but has something to do with cutting, clothing or trimming. The speculation is they refused to go along with the beards worn by the Orthodox with some saying they cut the beard off and others saying they refused to cut it off. These may have been focused on standards for their people to be set apart from the world.

Of greater importance they involved many low-ranking clergy and tradesmen. They also developed a church group both identifiable and with large number. They appear to be similar to other social revolutions later found across broader Europe such as the Lollards or Huguenots. They rejected the sacraments, monasticism, communion and ecclesiastical hierarchy. This revival lasted only about 100 years and may have merged into a Sect of Skhariya the Jew. This group renounced the doctrine of the Trinity and maintain some Jewish practices. It is said they deny the divinity of Christ but that may have just been an accusation. They would seem to have related with the idea of messianic Jews today. The reference to them being Jews was more of a derogatory term used by their opponents and most of the followers had been out of the Russian Orthodox Church.

Now this lends two important aspects to our reflection on this era and they are; such movements created churches that may have been teaching something slightly less but more Biblical also in the Russian Orthodox Church one might find a priest that discovered the truth and was preaching the full truth to a small congregation.

## Tolstoyan

Leo Tolstoy created a communal society that would devote itself to the study of the ministry of Jesus and especially the Sermon on the Mount. He developed a view that would be similar to the Baptist later in the United States concerning individual conscience espoused by Roger Williams. It is written that he expressed "great joy" that communes were being developed across his nation, in various parts of Europe, America and the world that agreed with his views. He was a harsh critic of the Russian Orthodox Church, a pacifist who questioned the concept of government and believed in a personal relationship as Christians with the teaching of the Bible.

Of greater importance, he wrote "'To speak of Tolstoyism,' to seek guidance, to inquire about my solution to questions, is a great and gross error. There has not been, nor is there any "teaching" of mine. There exists only the one and eternal universal teaching of the Truth, which for me, for us, is especially clearly expressed in the Gospels... I advised this young lady to live not by my conscience, as she wished, but by her own."

These communes all across Russia challenging people to think independently, to reject formalism and to simply seek truth and the word of God would provide a seedbed for which revival would later spring forth in Russia. For

Russians that challenge evangelical movements in their country as not being Russian, is to say, "Tolstoy is not Russian."

## Molokan

The Molokans are one of my favorite groups from a word that means milk drinker with milk being such an incredibly common word in Russian. The dating of this unusual teaching will begin very early with the Nestorians practicing milk drinking at about 1000 A.D. This would place it as old as the Russian Orthodox Church itself, and interesting enough, the group still exists to this day with some groups located in the southwestern part of the United States. Like so many groups before them, their opponents meant the title to be derogatory, but they took it and celebrated it by declaring themselves to be "drinking of the spiritual milk of God (according to first Peter 2:2)." They preferred to call themselves the Spiritual Christians. They rejected the Russian Orthodox Church, most Protestants and the Roman Catholic Church. They had a council of elders, sort of a Brat Soviet. Each church seems to be autonomous and therefore one might suspect a wide variety and doctrinal teachings one from the other. They would loosely be similar to Quakers and Mennonites and would've had spiritual services. Many of them are given the titles of Leapers and Jumpers indicating wild exuberance of worship. We know that in the early 1800s there were clearly reports of the outpouring of the Holy Spirit with speaking in tongues recorded among these congregations in revivals but lacked detail as to how far back in their history this went.

## Doukhobor

The Spirit Warriors of Christ is a group that is clearly identified in the 18th century, however, many believe it may go back to at least the 1500s. They were incredibly Bible centered and rejected the idea of state involvement in matters of faith and believed that they needed to struggle internally with their own beliefs as they found them in the word of God. They tended to call themselves "God's People" or "Christian." Opponents would make fun of them saying they were wrestling against God, but they would say they were wrestling together with God, or on God's side.

Interestingly, later many of these will be exiled to the Vyborg region. This would be at the turn-of-the-century about 1800 with 90 being exiled there and may have provided a seedbed for revival that would be there later with A. D. Urshan. The 1st Alexander would offer them a relocation program to avoid persecution and help in settling new lands and they would accept it. There would be exiles of these people over and over, but they remain one of the groups clearly identifiable and in existence for hundreds of years. Persecution under the czar was horrible for these people and in the final major exile coming in 1897 the Russian government permitted the group to leave for Canada with the agreement they would never return, they would migrate at their own expense and their leaders that were in jail would have to serve their sentence before being allowed to leave. These were the harsh conditions in the time of the Czar. They rejected state government, the Russian Orthodox Church, the priests, the icons, the Trinity and according to their accusers would have had a very low Christology. They were pacifist and this together with the rejection of state involvement in religion brought about the most severe persecution as it threatened the monarchy.

## Subbotniks

The term simply means "Sabbath keepers" and I would suspect there have been such as far back as the early days of the church itself when of course even the apostles would've been in this group. The Judaizing form of Christianity and therefore the doctrines may have varied as do all the churches in your town today. In Russia it may have been more pronounced than we have seen an expression of it elsewhere and this is because Judaism was tolerated under the czars. Therefore, difficult to sort out as these were being seen as Jewish, providing a haven for dissidents to practice their faith. In Russia they rejected the doctrine of the Trinity, accepted the Jewish Bible and observed the Sabbath. Of the one group in Moscow, it is said that they did not circumcise and believed in Jesus as a saint or a prophet. Others (like those that settled in Seattle, Washington) believe that Jesus is the Messiah and is the son of God and are waiting for his soon return. Of others, it is said they believed in the Christian Gospels and the fulfillment of Old Testament. Reading about such groups is very difficult because of the person writing about them and not having firsthand knowledge. About our view, what is important is the dissident protest rejecting Russian Orthodox Teachings and that it is widespread. There would be a great deal more individual thought in these groups and across these groups than would be found in the Russian Orthodox Church. This provides the likelihood that with the rejection of the Trinity and with a firm belief in the Scripture, that there would be those congregations that undoubtedly would have discovered the importance of the Holy Ghost and baptizing in His Name.

## The Peasant Revolt

To understand what is happening across the world and in Russia, we will for a while move outside of Russia starting in England and look at the development of the Reformation and the Radical Reformation which will sweep all across Europe producing one of the largest Democratic kingdoms to ever exist. This kingdom was on Russia's doorstep including many countries that Russia considered their territory today and providing the conversion of the Czar himself.

In the 1300s following the black plague, which itself had produced extreme religious zealousness as people sought answers from God, there arose preaching of what is termed "Liberal Theology." I remember years ago, at Harvard, the first time someone referred to me as a liberal theologian and with my Midwest background, I was shocked. He took time to explain to me that there were three basic political/religious/social forms of thinking with one being the state church and salvation via the institution, the second being the elect and the third that salvation was available to the whosoever will accept. The prevailing view at that time had been state church with this symbiotic relationship between the King and the Pope. These two powers controlled the lives of most people and held the masses in serfdom.

John Ball is an example of preachers, at that time, that were in the background preaching a certain truth like the Molokans in Russia. There is no telling how many Bible-based, seekers of truth were out preaching a message contrary to the state doctrine. These were people that were seeking a knowledge of the word of God. John Ball was what we would call today an evangelist. Traveling and preaching, a roving preacher, or what they called in those days "a hedge priest." He preached to the masses in the "common tongue," rather than Latin. He preached to the rebels waging the Peasant Revolt in an open-air meeting, and we have the following recorded from his sermon:

> "When Adam delved and Eve span, who then was the gentleman? From the beginning of all men by nature were created alike, and our bondage or servitude came in by unjust oppression of naughty men. For if God would have had any bondsman from the beginning, He would have appointed who should be bond and who free. And I therefore exalt you to consider that now the time has come, appointed to us by God, in which ye may (if ye will) cast off the yoke of bondage, and recover liberty."

This would produce a firestorm that would sweep the world. Eventually producing not only the democracy we enjoy today in which we hear the same phrases and ideology in our Declaration of Independence, but in questioning the state/church relationship cracking the door to open thinking about the Scripture and salvation. We would eventually all be seen by many such as most evangelicals, as the children of God and all having rights given to us by that God from the beginning. A loving God that died on the cross for our salvation, gave us His Spirit and Name.

## Lollards

John Ball was a Lollard which were traveling evangelists going across the English countryside like other groups such as the Huguenots in France and others stretching out across Europe preaching independent thinking that would affect not only society but religious thinking. This group was a result of the thinking of John Wycliffe who was a professor at the University of Oxford in England. There is a word in Dutch that is *lollen*, which means a mumbler. I would like to think this has something to do with speaking in tongues, but no one is certain why they have this title. He was going to produce a translation of the Scripture and he and the group would boldly challenge the state church by, what they called, "The Twelve Conclusions" and a much larger challenge all of which they will nail to the door of Westminster. His followers would fan out across the countryside preaching against the state church and questioning basic tenants of belief such as transubstantiation, challenging the office of the Pope and even equating the Pope as the antichrist. From this it raises the question of confessions to the priest as unnecessary to salvation. One of their great contributions was for church services and the Bible to be in a common language of the people.


## Erasmus

Desiderius Erasmus or the more general, one name, Erasmus was born in 1466 and will be a pivotal personage in the development of civilization. My old teacher friend George Williams of Harvard Divinity School in his book, "The Radical Reformation", refers to Erasmus as "Erasmus of Rotterdam, Oxford, Cambridge, Basel, Freiberg: Patron of Evangelicals in Spain and of Radicals Everywhere, though by Him Disowned." I was humored when I read this, because I felt this was absolutely a two-way street. He is used of God to bring about an incredible social revolution that in its ultimate conclusion will produce the Oneness Pentecostal Churches, democracy, the United States of America and a very human way of thinking about the condition of others. He will be one of those socially prominent individuals of the dark ages that was a brilliant thinker. As my brother Tim says, "He had a way of saying things humorously, that appeared to be a joke, so that it did not offend the King and others and yet it was the truth and caused people to think." I suppose that would make him somewhat of a Will Rogers of his day.

Erasmus himself will seemingly not be a true believer and he will not join the religious and social revolution that he spawned and spurred. On the surface what he did seemed quite simple, and that is, from the text that he had to work with. He questioned I John 5:7 which many had seen as a Trinitarian statement. In questioning it, he left it out of the text of the Bible he translated. What this did was challenge everything. Everyone had lived under the throne and altar system believing it was the institution that saved you and that by being obedient to the church and the King you would be saved by virtue of their office. To American Christians, this would be somewhat shocking today with our individualism and our personal relationship with Jesus Christ. To even question threatened everything. He produced the questions "Ought we to think for ourselves? Was it better to obey God rather than men? Did the church know what it was talking about?"

This questioning would not only produce democracy and Christian humanism, but also it would open the door for personal conscience and religion. It will produce the Reformation and more importantly the Radical Reformation. On society there will be great turbulence and within two or three centuries there will be the collapse of monarchies and state churches will lose their power. This change will cause the Peasant Revolt and have a liberation theology that will sweep the world. I must emphasize that through it a great Holy Ghost, One God, Jesus name Revival will be produced, but that is only part of this overwhelming story that will bless us all in so many ways. This is important to us apostolic's that hold the view that we do, to understand that the questioning of the Trinity will change all of society for the better. We will see that the questioning of the Trinity will ultimately produce the

Lithuanian – Polish Commonwealth which was the largest country in Europe and had a form of democracy. This questioning would ultimately produce The United States of America and other democracies and would shake Russia. I do not want to overstate the case and I am not saying the rejection of the Trinity will produce all of this, but rather the questioning will change society.

## The Reformation

The Reformation will give us a host of new individuals which will include Martin Luther and John Calvin. We will see how the questioning of the Trinity will be so prevalent that John Calvin will be accused of it and will defend an anti-Trinitarian position and in Transylvania, ultimately, the Lutheran Bishop will be a Unitarian.

Martin Luther was a Roman Catholic priest and saw himself as a Romanist until the day he died. He questioned, protested and sought to change many things in the Roman church but at the same time still tried to maintain a state church worldview. He is typical of so many affected by the preached word of his day. They made changes but only small incremental changes. He did strongly support justification by faith and many tenants of the changes that were coming. Reformation is a good term for such men as they were restricted to simply trying to reform their church. I personally have little interest in men such as Luther or Calvin because they are what I consider the showman of their day and simply in a very imperfect and poor manner reflected the deeper movement of the day. We see in them a popularity of compromise rather than the real change taking place. They are a watered-down illusion. The real heroes are likely names we will never hear and small churches, in rural areas preaching what the world will consider to be a radical idea that will bring about real change in the world, in society, in the church and in the hearts of men and women.

Such men are going to provide influence and thinking in a new way that men had not thought before. They will champion the idea of a certain openness. For example, the word preached in a common language, and the Bible available to all men and women. They will reject some ideas such as celibacy, but all of these are for the most part simply trying to reform the system.

More importantly, their minds and ideas will be changed at the very core without realizing it. The very idea that Luther would debate the papal authority, question tenets of the faith and make changes without hierarchal approval will all be to the revolution of the day that is bringing about real change on their conception. It is happening to them and they are not even aware. This movement is so pro-biblical, antiestablishment and questioning such tenants as the Trinity. They will actually speak out against such doctrines. In a recorded sermon by Martin Luther he will say, "it is indeed true that the name 'Trinity' is nowhere found in the Holy Scripture but has been conceived and invented by man." (From a sermon recorded in, *The Sermons of Martin Luther,* John Lenker, editor, volume 3, 1988, page 499.) Again, I want to make it very clear that I am not saying that Luther rejected the Trinity or broke with real Roman teaching, but the winds of change were forcing him to speak in a manner questioning even the basic teaching of the Roman Catholic Church and his view of the Trinity. If carefully examined, this will be slightly different than that of the Roman Catholic view of which he was likely a member.

## John Calvin

John Calvin while worshiped and adored by his followers in an almost cult like fashion, both in his time and today, reflects the struggles of that age in which church leaders, such as himself, are trying to hold on to the throne altar, the Roman Catholic Church and at the same time hold two divergent views. He will develop a theology that is so radically different than the past that it will create a third stream of politics and religion. Because it is a personality cult, he will be all over the place. For example, one moment shouting against the Trinity, and the next putting a man to death for opposing the Trinity doctrine.

He will take biblical words and biblical thoughts and turn them into a new system. Calvin will speak of predestination and the elect. Not unlike the throne and altar system, where the King is ruling by divine right, there will be this new system of the elect and the elders and the view that God has given the elect salvation, a covenant and therefore they are free to govern. We must understand the world in which they lived. It being spelled out that the king ruled by divine right and therefore everything was his. Silly things of which we would not think such as who had a right to hunt and fish or who had a right to gather sticks in the great forest. Calvin would now transfer these rights, not to all men, but only the elect. It would be left to the radical reformers and Bible believers to champion the idea of liberal theology to the point that all men could be saved and that all men could hunt and fish, even own rifles one day and gather sticks in the great forest.

Calvin would institute this form of government at Geneva with harsh treatments of those that broke the smallest of rules and a man could be put to death simply for his belief and in his thinking. Why not? They were not the elect, had no rights and were going to spend eternity in hell anyway. Nevertheless, he is caught up in this wide sweep of anti-Trinitarians and social reform challenging the state institutions. He will himself be charged repeatedly for his lack of Trinitarian statements. Caroli will charge him as a non-Trinitarian and say that he does not use the word Trinity nor the word persons in reference to God.

**The Radical Reformation**

Evangelical Christians – Baptist in Russia on its webpage, "Evangelical Baptist movement in Russia was a great spiritual heritage of the Radical Reformation, which proclaimed the forgotten teaching of the Gospel on justification through faith. This movement stepped forward towards reaching the goal set by the Reformation – revival of the early Christianity of apostolic times." Wow, this is an incredibly true statement, and I do believe they believe it with all their heart, but when it is analyzed it will be rejected by many of them even though it has shaped their theology and is at the core of their teaching. The single biggest common denominator among the Radical Reformers is the rejection of the doctrine of the Trinity and yes it was doing exactly what this webpage says it did which was to push the movement forward towards early Christianity and apostolic times.

In understanding Russia, and the many revivals that will take place in Russia, we can see them more clearly by analyzing them in other countries such as Poland and surrounding areas. There will be one revival after another that will take place in countries such as Transylvania in which the King himself will become a convert. This will then have an influence on the Ukraine and from there spread into Russia. Over and over we will see revivals take place and spread into Russia where the Czar, Alexander I, will mentally be converted.

A significant group that will have a tremendous impact on the later Pentecostal movement will be the Mennonites which will be invited by Catherine the Great to immigrate into the Volga region. Many of those will later come to the United States and in turn spread a revival here. Among those being invited in will be the Mennonites which will produce a seedbed to produce the Anabaptists in Russia and will later be confused with the Baptist in America, but more properly ought to be called The Christian Evangelicals.

There has been spiritual revival after spiritual revival all across the territories that were the Soviet Union with groups constantly being sent into exile and moved from one portion of the country to another.  It is important to understand that the Anabaptists of Europe are not the same as the Baptist of America. Also, the Pentecostals of this region in Europe have a very different history and background than the Pentecostals of America.

This chapter was not written to indicate that these are the total of all the revivals that happened in the area we called the Soviet Union, but it is simply to show that we have some history of revivals happening there just as they happened in other places in the world and affected people such as Alexander 1 of Russia.

## Chapter Three

## The Apostolic Faith and Andrew David Urshan

Brother Urshan is credited with beginning the present-day revival in Russia and the region. Of course, the Apostolic Faith has always existed from the beginning of the church and this is true worldwide. We speak of him as a beginning in the same manner that we might speak of Azusa Street or Frank Ewart. There is a present-day revival that is quite exceptional, and Brother Urshan is the spark that brought it about in that region. He is quite exceptional because he is not only a pioneer of the One God Jesus name revival but is the forerunner for the Pentecostal movement itself in that area. Brother Urshan while being a pioneer in Russia holds the same position in the United States of America.

Andrew David Urshan was born in Iran in a little village of Abajaloo which is in the Ararat Plaines in the region of what is today Iran very close to Turkey and Armenia. Despite his humble beginnings, he is going to become conversant in both Russian and English. Such men put many of us to shame as he will write five books, publish a magazine and write songs all in his secondary language. Generally, the family preferred to be noted as Persian and because he will be persecuted, as many of his relatives were and they were killed for this fact, he deserves to be separated from the general population of Iran. Like Abraham he will be called out of this country to do a great work.

(FORM NO. 1730.—CONSULAR.)
(Corrected February, 1913)

Fee for Passport ............ $1.00
Fee for administering oath and
preparing passport application. 1.00

# EMERGENCY PASSPORT APPLICATION.

## NATURALIZED

No. *11* *Andrew D. Urshan* Issued, ........................., A NATURALIZED AND LOYAL CITIZEN OF THE UNITED STATES, hereby apply to the American *Legation* at *Teheran, Persia* for an emergency passport for myself, accompanied by my wife, ........................., and minor children, as follows: ........................., born at ......................... on the ......................... day of ........................., ; and .........................

I solemnly swear that I was born at *Urumia, Persia* on or about the *17* day of *May*, *1884*; that I emigrated to the United States, sailing on board the *Hamburg* from *Hamburg, Germany* on or about the *1st* day of *October*, *1901*; that I resided *11½* years, uninterruptedly, in the United States, from *1901* to *1913* at *Chicago, Ill.* that I was naturalized as a citizen of the United States before the *U.S. District* Court of *Cook County*, at *Chicago, Ill.* on the *4th* day of *June*, *1912* as shown by the accompanying Certificate of Naturalization; that I am the bearer of Passport No. *17167* issued by *Department of State*, on the *22nd* day of *October*, *1913*, which is returned herewith; that I am the identical person referred to in said certificate and passport; that I am domiciled in the United States, my permanent residence therein being at *Chicago*, in the State of *Illinois*, where I follow the occupation of *Preacher*; that I have been residing abroad temporarily since *Oct. 12, 1913* in the following countries: *London, England, 2 months and Urumia, Persia, since March 1, 1914* that I last left the United States on the — day of *November*, 1913, arriving in *London, England*, the — day of *December*, 1913; that I am now temporarily residing at *Tabriz, Persia*; and that I intend to return to the United States within *one* months with the purpose of residing and performing the duties of citizenship therein.

I have not applied elsewhere for a United States passport or for consular registration and been refused.

I desire the passport for the purpose of *immediate return to the United States.*

### OATH OF ALLEGIANCE.

Further, I do solemnly swear that I will support and defend the Constitution of the United States against all enemies, foreign and domestic; that I will bear true faith and allegiance to the same; and that I take this obligation freely, without any mental reservation or purpose of evasion: So help me God.

*Andrew D. Urshan*

American *Consulate* at *Tabriz, Persia*
Sworn to before me, this *12* day of *August* 1915

*Gordon Paddock*
American *Consul.*

*See circular instructions concerning the Expatriation Act of March 2, 1907.* (OVER.)

60

R.M.S. "Lusitania"

Andrew David Urshan and Russian Apostolic believers in St. Petersburg.

Andrew David Urshan was born in 1885 and raised in a Presbyterian family and his religious experience is varied depending on who is discussing it. Urshan always spoke of being saved when he was a Presbyterian, however according to his testimony, the Russians say he did not become a true Christian until he came to America. Many, now days, in the Apostolic Movement would say he had some religious experience even before he came to America. He, likely, would not have thought of himself as a Presbyterian. Presbyterian missionaries were very active, often in schools and hospitals. The lasting effect of Protestant missionary work among the Muslims will be institutions such as the American University in Beirut. He would have seen himself culturally as a Christian. This meaning he was not a Muslim, and these are often distinctions of identity rather than deeply held faith. He did have a deep and abiding faith in God and a personal relationship. He talked with God and God talked with him.

There is some small difference as to exactly when he came to America. Writers here are saying in 1901 and the Russians recording it as 1902. Andrew David seems to have fled to the United States as there is some rumor or scandal associated with his departure and his parents raising money quickly to get him out of the area. These rumors, which were probably lies, will haunt him on his return. This situation is referred by him and those that record in Russian of his ministry. The details are never given. This no doubt would make him all the lonelier in the United States of America.

At only 16 or 17 years of age he arrived in the United States of America with no knowledge of our language or customs and will rely heavily on God as his help. He will secure a job and will eventually become a waiter. He will be quite proud that he was noted for doing good work. Try and place the setting in the first years of 1900. A rather grimy New York in the mass influx of immigrants mostly from Europe and Eastern Europe flooding into Ellis Island. Picture if you will the shortage of jobs, the poor lifestyle and the difficulty that immigrants had at that time. Let your mind picture a 16-year-old boy with all the hardships connected with it. He was a stranger in a strange land.

On January 1, 1901 a lady by the name of Agnes Ozman received the Holy Ghost in Bible school in Topeka Kansas headed by Charles Parham. Parham had been preaching for several years the need of a fresh restoration of the church that he called The Apostolic Faith Movement. He had been preaching and praying for the miracles and blessings of the New Testament and for the baptism of the Holy Ghost. He had asked the question how we will know it when people get the Holy Ghost and a former missionary had told him that on the foreign fields it was not uncommon to see people blessed and speaking in other tongues. This makes clear that this new fresh revival was simply an extension of what God was already doing and had done in every century of the church, but this was far more expansive than had been seen since the days of Pentecost. This Pentecostal Revival or Apostolic Faith Movement was in its embryonic stage as Urshan arrives in the United States. Coming from Iran, which even in those days had little toleration for

Christianity, he had received good training from his parents and a Presbyterian school. Like many immigrants coming to the United States from such a limited Christian background, they assumed that all those that say they are Christian are in fact dedicated Bible believers with a strong commitment to Jesus. He was shocked to go to church and find that some were those that went to church on Sunday but drank and danced during the week and he began to search for churches that were a little more Bible centered. Finding the Baptist and evangelicals he began to worship with them. He was particularly attracted to the ministry of D. L. Moody and began to worship with members of this group. There was a strong Persian group associated with Moody Bible Institute of which he seemed to be a leader in 1908. Among these Persians, God poured out the Holy Ghost speaking in tongues and by 1909 A. D. Urshan was among their number. Soon afterwards this group urged him to become the pastor of the Persian mission in Chicago in 1910. He will prefer the title, "The Persian Evangelist," the rest of his life.

Now active in the Pentecostal movement, Andrew David Urshan becomes a leader and a prominent evangelist. He will be seen at most significant events such as the Apostolic Worldwide Meeting in Los Angeles and the formation of the Assemblies of God in Hot Springs, Arkansas. At this point the Jesus name revival is beginning and is what the opponents will call the New Issue. This has a traumatic effect on Brother Urshan. He views the Pentecostal movement being torn apart over a doctrinal issue that he is not quite certain is that important. He will in fact write

letters condemning the Jesus name people or at least urging them not to be divisive. This

may be hard for people to understand today looking back and some may condemn him for not taking a bolder stand on Jesus name baptism, but to me it indicates the honesty and sincerity of this person that is struggling with an issue and does not want it to hurt the overall move of God that is taking place in America. He does believe in baptism in Jesus name and takes pride in the fact that he himself had already been doing this for as early as 1910, but without any special significance as to its meaning. This is a real turmoil and struggle and reflects the turmoil and struggle of that time.

In my mind two-men stand out. E. N. Bell and Andrew David Urshan. Bell will start out Trinitarian as the head of the Assembly of God and will write articles in their magazine and plead for a revelation of Jesus as the one true God and baptism in his name. He will be baptized in Jesus name himself, but eventually will turn back and stay with the Trinitarians. Andrew David Urshan will do just the opposite as he will start out somewhat Jesus name himself and will then plead for everyone to stay together even if it means compromising the message. He will then be baptized in Jesus name and begin to teach others starting in Russia and then coming home to be a pioneer of this group in the United States. I am showing this to explain to everyone on all sides just how turbulent this was in the early days of the Pentecostal movement.

Brother Urshan decided to return home to his village in 1914, and this may be partly to escape the turmoil in the United States, but also with a burden and a drive for missions. He does not realize how broadly God is going to use him as he thinks and sees himself as a Persian minister returning home to Persia to preach to his own, but God has bigger plans for him. He will become an international evangelist. There is an irony in that he will describe his preaching in Petrograd as that of Philip "preaching the kingdom of God and the name of Jesus". The irony is that just as Philip the persecution is pushed into Samaria, so will Urshan be pushed into Armenia, Georgia, Russia, Estonia and Finland. He will for the early days of the Pentecostal revival be one of the most significant international evangelists on the scene and will not only preach the

Pentecostal message but will introduce apostolic doctrine and as a result the Apostolic Pentecostal message will dominate the Pentecostal revival in the Soviet Union from 1917 until about 1926.

Andrew Urshan will return to his village in present-day Iran close to a village then called Uremia (present day Resaine). This small region of Persia or Iran was unique because it was populated by people of many nations including Kurds, Arabs, Persians and Turks with all the various religious views. This was a blessing in the fact that there had been general tolerance because of the diversity but it was a hotbed getting ready to explode. This region of the world was jointly administered by the British Empire and Imperial Russia.

Young Andrew David expected to be greeted with a warm welcome on his return as generally a son of the village returning from a far distant land would be received. The village elders came to see him, and he anticipated that they would throw a celebration in his honor, but the old rumors prevailed. Instead he is met with hostility and they do not want to hear from him or about his new-found faith. He tries to preach a little but there are great threats and his parents plead with him to remain silent. He spends long hours in prayer and God speaks to him and tells him that he will have a revival. He remained silent for two months and writes articles and submits them to be printed in a magazine by the Free Protestant Mission, but they are rejected. He himself feels rejected. During this time of silence one of those that had spread rumors on him died suddenly. He begins to be more aggressive by openly praying at his house, in the streets, in the fields and everywhere. Praying and praying openly and people seeing it, little by little the village begins to change.

He schedules another service and this time people respond and he is not opposed. People began to see miracles healings, and people receiving the Holy Ghost including family members, villagers and more importantly people coming from other villages to hear him. The great revival that God had promised was becoming a reality.

He left America in 1914 and arrived in that region either sometime that year or early 1915. According to Russian records of the churches there, Urshan will spend almost a year in Iran and later a few months in Russia. He will hold lively enthusiastic meetings sharing the message of the Holy Ghost speaking in tongues with those in his village and around Iran. It was a time of great excitement but the unthinkable was on the horizon.

The Kurds went on a rampage and decided to commit genocide against all Armenians and Persians with other groups getting caught up and attacked as well. Only recently has Turkey openly admitted to this human rights violation on such a massive scale. It was horrible! Multitudes were put to death and whole villages wiped out. Brother Urshan would see his village destroyed and his mother would die not directly, but slowly as she administered to the needs of so many others. Before this rampage there will be about 600,000 Armenians living in this region and the immediate death toll will be 300,000 with hundreds of thousands more displaced and with tens of thousands dying from lack of food and exposure.

What will now take place will create a new word in the English language – genocide? Before Hitler tried to eliminate all Jews, the Ottoman Empire had embarked on a policy of destroying several subgroups, including Armenians, in their country. World War I was underway, and the Russians were aligned with the British as the Turks joined the opposition.

Refugees fleeing Iran

This provided a little cover in which Young Turks developed a plan and tried to eliminate anyone that was not like them. The Young Turks had come to power in 1908 in the

Ottoman Empire and they were extremely zealous for their religious view and ethnocentricity. They will then launch a series of attacks over different people killing over 300,000 between 1914 and 1920.

The First World War is a time of great instability that will eventually not only cause shockwaves in the Ottoman Empire but will eventually topple the Czar. It would be hard to imagine the turmoil that everyone is going through and the uncertainty from day-to-day. This will be felt later in Petrograd. Even the name Petrograd gives the instability of the time having been called St. Petersburg for so many years, but now that sounds to German and the name is changed for this brief period in history.

With this Armenian Genocide, there will be a smaller but very targeted and significant massacre in the Uremia Region of the Ottoman Empire in what is today Iran and it will be termed the Assyrian genocide. This fits with the testimony of a young Urshan. He speaks of a time of persecution and then it lets up and then again, the really bad attack takes place. This would've been the earlier attack against all Armenians and any others caught in the area. February 25, 1915 would have been the main assault on Uremia and the village from which the Urshan family came. It was undoubtedly completely destroyed. Assyrians would have been Christian in the general sense with a strong Presbyterian influence in the area. Of great note, a British report stated that many Muslim families in the area tried to hide and protect their Christian neighbors while many hid them in their homes.

The aftermath of this persecution is that in Uremia and the region, 4000 will die of sickness, hunger and exposure. Our brother mentions in his book that his mother did not die directly from the attack but gave her life ministering to others in the village. She is part of that subsequent death toll.

I personally believe there is a spiritual aspect to this point in history that will be seen in World War I and again in World War II. It is from the Jewish people that the Messiah was to be born and thus the devil hates the Jewish people. Armenia is the first nation to officially declare itself a Christian nation and claims the Apostolic Church, (not to be confused with our Apostolic Church), and the Assyrians had early on converted to Christianity. It is this spirituality that has caused the devil to stir people up and target them over and over. There is a saying among the Arabs, speaking of Iraq and Iran, that it is The Throne of All Troubles. An evangelical might say the devil has a strong hold on this area and does not want to let it go. Remember these villages and this area was noted for being homogeneous with many ethnic groups and religions all accepting each other. It is this aspect that the Ottomans and the Young Turks hate. People loving each other and living together.

Refugees fleeing Turkey and Iran.

Thanks to the Russians and their sacrificial effort of saving what documents they could through a horrible time of decades of persecution, we have his testimony in his own words. "During those horrible days of murder, bloodshed, hunger, disease and death many mourners in Persia turn to the throne of Mercy. From the whole nation God heard prayers to Him. So, he sent fear to the Turks and Kurds fled when the Russian army returned to Uremia. Christians dispersed in various parts started to return to their homes and villages destroyed by the Muslims. Screams, cries and tears were heard all around, for everything was destroyed or stolen and there were corpses everywhere. Suddenly there were credible shouts of joy, people saw the Russian army returning to the blood – covered streets of Uremia. We resume our meetings [preaching] in the streets. Many people were agitated and full of vengeance toward the remaining Muslims. We talked to the people and make them not to hate the enemy for the Spirit of Christ teaches us to forgive."

A.D. Urshan was able to minister in Iran at this point, and it was a time of great spiritual harvest as people turn to God. In 1915 the Russian army was recalled home and there began a new stage of persecution. He was in a band of villagers' believers and relatives that made their way to Georgia for safety. There again he was able, in a limited fashion, to minister. It was against the law for foreign preachers to minister in Russia and anything that was not Russian Orthodox tended to be persecuted. Anything else is called a sect. Now this sort of name calling has very little effect on Americans as we simply laugh it off while considering the person calling such to be ignorant, but in Russia such a title has a deep negative meaning to the general population. Despite all of this, God gave him grace and he was able to preach and hold baptisms. There was at that time a rather large population of Persians and no doubt Armenians that were fleeing the genocide. This provided him with a rather large group of people to minister to which the Russian government likely had little concern.

It is hard for us as Americans to understand the situation as it existed in Russia but in their mind, the Russian is to be Russian Orthodox and that is pretty much the limit of their great concern. It is not to say that they do not do mission work, and in the past, they did try to recruit, but for the most part they are content to simply deal with the Russians. Therefore, other ethnic groups would likely have the opportunity of hearing him preach. Still after all these years, the Russians still speak of the great revival that was had in Georgia.

Andrew David Urshan is now 30 years of age and in the prime of his strength. He is a citizen of the United States of America. Even in that day to be a US citizen provided great protection and freedom. In all the turmoil he had lost his documents and was an undocumented alien in Imperial Russia. There was a United States Consulate in Tiflis and he was able to establish himself to the degree that he was granted a temporary visa and passport for a limited time, but then needed to return to the United States to establish his permanent credentials.

The Free Protestant Mission had taken on the task of ministering to so many of those that had been displaced by the onslaught of the Kurds. This was a group that had significant standing in that region. The Free Protestant Mission received Brother Urshan as an evangelist and preacher and, they opened their doors to him.

Picture if you will, Andrew David Urshan, not the elderly statesman with a thick accent that most of us remember. Picture him in his prime, looking perhaps much like his great-grandson Joel Urshan. Picture him the perfect evangelist, 30 years of age, dark, lean, handsome and single. He would've had a little mustache, dark black hair, wearing a collar popular in the early 1900s that stands up with the corners simply turned down a little then a black bow tie. In Russia he would've worn a heavy wool black coat that came down past the knees and not your typical Russian fur hat, but a fur hat that would have looked more like the caps worn by American soldiers in WWII. He was perfect for the gospel and excited about the message he was preaching. Urshan is a widely traveled urbane sophisticate by this time. His preaching no doubt is peppered with his many experiences. He has traveled to the United States of America and has become a citizen and has adapted to life in New York City. He has now returned, traveling across the ocean, and has seen the horrors of war and now he has moved further north from Iran to Armenia, Georgia, to the lower regions of Russia and soon will travel to the North. Think of the experiences that he must share and remember there are no televisions, few radios and he is a firsthand witness to history.

While all the rest of this is true that being his strength and good looks and being such an interesting person with whom to visit, I do not want to minimize the fact that he is deeply dedicated and passionate about the work of God. Long intensive daily prayer sessions that is the standard in that region and is experienced with the Holy Ghost of which he is a witness and his sacrificing and giving all to the work of God, it boggles the mind how he survived and was able to move around and accomplish as much as he did in such a short time. No doubt he had brought some money with him from America and that the Pentecostal churches who were dedicated to global evangelism would no doubt have given him some money, but there must've been a point where he was simply surviving on faith and faith alone. The mail would've been slow and even if people wanted to send him money he would likely be back home before it arrived. He must have received some free will offerings from preaching no doubt staying with people in their homes and receiving some help, but faith had to be the key ingredient.

We can follow his track North by the places he preached and the revivals he held. One of the most significant is Armavir and here his fervent preaching will spark such a revival that it will leave behind a rather significant church that is still there to this day. He is at this point still preaching a Trinitarian message and baptism, and as a result the churches will be Christian Evangelical Pentecostal. In these churches his picture will hang as the person that first brought them the message of the Holy Ghost. Because of these great Evangelical/Pentecostal revivals the notoriety of him begins to spread and the Free

Protestant Missions open their doors to him to come and preach and he is invited especially to Vyborg.

I often ponder the exact route and means by which Andrew David Urshan traveled across Russia. We know of his great success in Georgia and the Krasnodar Region of southern Russia. Remember this is where we started with Noah at the beginning of the book and like Noah, he is starting his journey here following much the same trail. Next, we know he is invited to Vyborg which is close to what is today St. Petersburg and Finland. How did he get from the South to the North and did he preach his way in churches of the Free Protestant Mission? Given the time element, we can make certain suppositions because he was only in the country for a few months and this would certainly rule out walking to the North or spending much time going from church to church.

You can look on the map and there is a road that is pretty much due North from the places he preached in the South to where he preached in the North. There were so few cars in those days. The Russian roads have never been good, so it is highly unlikely he was driven or took a bus. He could've gone by boat up the Volga River and passed through Volgograd, but the most likely form of transportation would have been rail. This has long been the standard form of transportation in Russia and has been subsidized by the governments so that it is relatively cheap for him to travel. The cheapest way would have been to sit on a bench or a stool in an open car perhaps sleeping on the floor over this long trip. He likely would have passed through Volgograd,

Kazan and Moscow coming to Petrograd where he could've caught a train or bus to Vyborg. This would have been hard traveling but not nearly as hard as the things he had been through in his life. In fact, a train ride might've seemed very luxurious to him.

I have never heard of any connection with him in these major cities and especially Moscow? There is no doubt many reasons why he would not have preached in the cities. Cities are highly organized with a strong central government and an active secret police and they would have wanted to maintain the purity of Russia and the Imperial government. Even today the mayors of these cities function at times in an almost autonomous way, making their own laws and restricting outsiders. There would have been the fact that the city itself was so overwhelming you could get lost trying to find your way around and locating small bands of evangelicals. It is even more likely that because he has an invitation from The Free Protestant Mission in Vyborg that he simply heads directly there. He is a man on a mission. In addition, there is the fact that he decided to return to the United States from Petrograd via England and therefore had to move rather quickly to not overstay his temporary papers.

Vyborg is the divinely ordained spot that Andrew David needs to be at this moment. It puts him in close proximity to Finland, Estonia and Petrograd. It is divinely ordained because this is a more intellectually open area than much of the rest of the nation. It is divinely ordained because hungry souls are waiting here. It is divinely ordained because here Urshan will meet the exact leaders needed for the future revival.

It is important to understand that the Pentecostal revival and the Apostolic Church are homegrown revivals. He will be given credit for bringing the Jesus name message and he will be seen as the forerunner of the Pentecostal revival. But, the Holy Ghost revival had started before he arrived. How did this happen? The answer is," in so many ways." It is recorded that Russian sailors received the Holy Ghost at Azusa Street in California. Spirit filled pastors in Germany and Poland were already preaching this message and more than one Russian pastor had received the Holy Ghost and was preaching the same. Finally, it is a sovereign work of the Holy Ghost itself.

The Russians have been very good about preserving the testimonies of various leaders and church members and they have written a book, **The Chronicle.** To me it is like a testimony service as they have saved various accounts and snippets and put them together. It is like a testimony service in which A. D. Urshan steps up shares an experience and then Bishop Somordin or his wife stands and testifies and then Pastor Ivanov gives a testimony and then another. One account that is very interesting tells of a man whose name is forgotten but is only described as someone from Finland visiting the church and I want to share that testimony with you.

> *"In March 1914, a visiting brother from Finland was speaking on a Thursday meeting. During his sermon his normal speech suddenly*

changed into a strange incomprehensible language. After his monologue, one of the sisters rose from her seat, walked up to the preacher and ask him: 'dear brother, do you know what you have just said in another time?' He replied that he did not, because the Lord had given him the gift of other tongues but not endowed him with the gift of interpretation. Then she told him that what he had said in fact was a fragment from Psalms 117, verses 17 to the end. Then he started reading those verses while he was reading, the Holy Spirit again started speaking through him and some new tongue. Then the sister again explained what he had said. It was the verses from Malachi 3:17, 3:18, 4:1, and 4:2. The Lords words directed at us were very comforting: "for behold, the day comes, burning like an oven, with all the arrogant and evil doers will be stubble; the date it comes she'll burn them up, says the Lord of hosts, so that it will leave them neither root nor branch. But for you fear my name the Sun of righteousness shall arise with healing in his wings. You shall go forth leaping like calves from the stall." These verses from the Bible were very serious and promised us beautiful blessings in the future. An equally strong was the joy that came the knowledge of the Lord's being with us and leading us in his true way. All that happened in the first *apostolic church was happening in our small congregation."*

This testimony makes two things clear and that is someone from Finland visiting the small congregation had spoken in tongues and more importantly, it was not a surprise to these people and an experience that they seem to understand and practice. They considered it to be apostolic and felt that their congregation was patterning itself after the New Testament and the time of the apostles. This would have been at least a year before Andrew David's visit.

According to the **Dictionary of Pentecostal and Charismatic Movements**, at least the following groups had received the Holy Ghost experience of speaking in tongues before Urshan's arrival. As early as 1907 there are reports of small Pentecostal congregations in Estonia which is likely to spill over from revivals in Scandinavia. Germans were preaching among German villages in the Ukraine as early as 1909. And a Pastor William Fetler was preaching in Russia several years before the Russian Revolution.

Some of those listed as preaching the Pentecostal message in Russia before 1915 are very significant names and yet many of us have never heard of them. One is Alexander Boddy of England born in 1854. He was trained formally in theology at Durham, England and must've studied under no less than J. B. Lightfoot who ordained him in 1884. Of great significance is the tremendous travel that this man engaged in going to Canada, Egypt, Africa, Palestine and of importance Russia. Because of his travels and his writings, he was given membership in the prestigious Royal Geographical Society and the Imperial Geographical Society of Russia. Boddy was influenced by Keswick. In 1907 he went to Oslo Norway to witness the Pentecostal revival led by T. B. Barrett and there received the baptism of the Holy Ghost. About this same time his wife Mary also received the Pentecostal experience as well as their daughters all speaking in tongues. Both these people would be great champions of the Pentecostal movement with Mary having been healed carrying on a very active healing ministry and laying hands on Smith Wigglesworth which received healing. Of interest, Urshan will meet Barrett in Oslo and exactly how this acquaintance was made is not clear, but likely some of those with the Pentecostal experience spoke of his teaching and preaching and that it spilled over into Russia with these two men of like faith wanting to get together to share with one another. We do know that from Oslo, Urshan went to London and there he met with the Boddys and ministered with them for several services. I would suspect that this was an introduction by Barrett.

Another linkage is Eleanor Patrick, an English woman who had been stirred and had a desire to be a revivalist preacher such as Torrey and Inwood. We might think of her as a Russian or English Aimee Semple McPherson. According to her own testimony, she received the Holy Ghost speaking in tongues during a meeting with A. A. Boddy in Hamburg in December 1908. She visited Russia in 1909 spending time in Revel (now Tallinn, Estonia), Riga and Dwinsk (now Daugavpils, Latvia) and Witevsk (Belarus). She seems to have Alexander A. Boddy as a supervisor or covering. E. Patrick claimed that 200 people were converted within two months of her ministry.

Patrick moved to Libau (now Liepaja) where the Town Council allowed her to use a hall with 700 seats free of charge. She also noted that a German evangelist, Eugen Edel, had preached in Riga and Libau. The report to Boddy: "H. Rabe (brother of Riga Rabe) is doing a wonderful work. He was converted and received his baptism in our Frankfurt work, and works in the power of the Spirit." Later Patrick moved further to Dwinsk and Witebsk then settling in Saratov, Russia. She would've had influence on Russia especially among the German-speaking, and the Holy Ghost message would have spread through this teaching. She is now directly in Russia about the time of A. D. Urshan. All of this is laying a great seedbed in which the apostolic message will grow. In fact, even the Trinitarian's will likely call themselves apostolic. This term has been segregated in the United States.

Another one mentioned earlier is William Fetler, well educated at Spurgeon College in England where he graduated in 1907. A Baptist minister, not truly Pentecostal, but heavily influenced by the movement and used his church and good offices to promote the Pentecostal message by inviting in Pentecostal speakers.

There is a wonderful article that you can find on the Internet entitled, "Origins of Pentecostalism in Latvia." It is written by Valdis Teraudkalns and gives us many names and the early days of Pentecost. One statement with which I strongly agree is, "Pentecostalism has often been viewed as an exotic export of foreign missionaries who came to disturb traditional religiosity. Looking at the wider context helps to show that Pentecostalism was born in Latvia in a time when it was no longer possible to speak about Latvia as ethnically, religiously or culturally monolithic. In fact, it is doubtful whether a golden age of homogeneity can ever be found. "Like Latvia, the Russian Church of the Apostolic Movement, or as is often called Pentecostalism must be seen as indigenous. It is homegrown and is for the most part a spontaneous revival of Russians responding to Russians.

This was God's timing, and God had brought his man to meet those leaders of importance that would carry on the church over the next several decades. Another statement that is true and with which I agree in Teraudkalns' article, "Early Pentecostals did not establish ecclesiastical organizations and therefore we cannot speak about Pentecostalism as firmly established in Latvia prior to The First World War." This would also be true of Russia and the truth be told, for the non-oneness groups it would be years after the war before they were organized. Here is where Andrew David Urshan will really make his mark.

The task of Brother Urshan as he came to this region was viewed by him as sharing the experience of the Holy Ghost, but God's plans for him were much broader. He was not here to bring the Pentecostal message but rather define, refine, and expand, and more importantly, he was here to introduce Jesus name baptism and the rudiments of the Apostolic message. This is a task that is way beyond him and the short time of his visit, but it is here in this region that he will introduce the message and meet and ordain the church leaders that will truly expand the truth.

This is not to minimize the great significance of Andrew David Urshan in Russia. He is a pioneer of the Pentecostal faith, and because he was Jesus name that message will dominate the Pentecostal revival for many years. When I say that the Pentecostal revival in Russia is homegrown I mean that there are two significant pioneers of the Pentecostal message and that being Andrew David Urshan and Ivan Voronaev. Even when we look at these two leaders we realize that they are children of this region simply coming home to share their testimony and as such it is a truly Russian Church. The reason I'm saying this is that the Pentecostal message is often depicted in that region as an American church, but the Apostolic Church of the New Testament is universal with roots planted in every nation. Seemingly this church would've developed if there had been no contact with the United States and we will see it established in Russia, by Russians with very little outside influence. For this reason, it will survive when cut off from the West.

Urshan is now at Vyborg, he was the guest of the Free Protestant Mission and we must remember this is a time in which there are no formal Pentecostal organizations, nor even Classic Pentecostal Congregations. While there is a formal group of the Free Protestants, this may be a more general term of simply evangelical churches that were into more of the proto-Pentecostal types. At any rate he is free to preach openly, and even the secret police attend his meetings to observe and report back favorably. It is here that he will meet two significant individuals, A. I. Ivanov and N. P. Somordin, and they will begin to preach and minister as a team. Here then is the embryo of the first Pentecostal organization or denomination in Russia, and will in fact give birth to organizations, The Christian Evangelical Church Pentecostal and The Christian Evangelical Church in the Spirit of the Apostles.

Now It can be argued that these two organizations are an outgrowth of the Christian Evangelical Church and to some degree that is true, but it is these men that will define both these new organizations. As Apostolic's it is difficult for us to realize, but here in America the Assembly of God is largely organized with leaders of the Oneness Movement and thus men such as Urshan are in fact founders of both the Trinitarian Pentecostal groups, as well as, the Oneness Pentecostal Organizations. They have a rightful place of recognition in both groups, and in the same way Andrew David Urshan is the founder of the Trinitarian Pentecostal Movement and the Oneness Pentecostal Church of Russia. In the latter he is going to be more significant because he is a founder of both, but the oneness message will dominate in all Pentecostal churches for the first couple decades and continues to have influence.

I can think of no individual that has a greater influence in the worldwide Pentecostal movement in its founding stage than is Andrew David Urshan. He is significant at not only preaching worldwide but is present in the forming of so many Pentecostal denominations as in Russia. The Assembly of God in the United States, The Pentecostal Assemblies of the World, The Apostolic Faith of Canada with Frank Small and so many others. He seems everywhere and extremely active in those early years. This is interesting because he is not often thought of as an organizational man. He is very open and ministers in all groups and does not seem concerned about holding positions. He is not out for himself but is willing to work hard for Jesus Christ and the truth. He sees the importance of a well-organized church group.

Andrew David Urshan will minister in Vyborg, Helsinki and possibly Estonia, but eventually will end in Petrograd where he will have his greatest influence. He ministers in Finland and people from Scandinavia will remember him, but he has great difficulty with the language. The cities in which Urshan will minister are significant populations and are all in Russian territory forming a circle around the Gulf of Finland. Vyborg is around 100 miles from Petrograd and is North and West of the city around the top of the Gulf. There is a nice highway here and following on down that road a little South you would come to Kotka, then driving on due South on the coast of the Gulf you would come to Helsinki; a short boat ride across the gulf almost directly east is Tallinn, Estonia. Now this will provide two possible means of transportation with the one being the highway and the other by boat. Each city mentioned is a port city. I've thrown Estonia in because in my memory it seems that I was told he visited there although there is no written record of this event. He could very easily have reached from one city to the next and then turned around and preached the same route back. He has a hard time with; Finnish, nevertheless his ministry there remained respected. Finland currently was part of the Imperial Russian Empire but all that is about to change. The people know that this area will soon be an autonomous country of its own and many Russian citizens fearing for their future begin to flood back toward Petrograd.

Urshan will learn Russian rather quickly and he would share his ministry in their native tongue. Arriving in Petrograd he will really strike fire holding meetings that will start with 25 persons and quickly grow to over 150. The meeting halls were often small, and people would gather in and must stand for three or four hours. Many asked to be baptized. The water was extremely cold; often covered with ice when they came forward for baptism. It is here that Urshan will come to terms with water baptism having the name of Jesus invoked over the baptized.

Too many times, the fact that one does not get an instantaneous revelation is seen to be a negative, but to me the fact that they had to wrestle with this makes this all the more significant. Following the timeline seems very interesting. Urshan had been baptizing in Jesus name beginning in 1910, and this was in the matter of doing it simply because the Bible said it and no particular thought given to it, nor baptizing this way exclusively. In 1913 at the Meeting in Los Angeles, Ewart and Cook and possibly Urshan heard of baptism in Jesus name. Now Andrew David said that Ewart and Cook had told him not to baptize in

Jesus name, and this would be consistent with their records as they had decided that baptizing in Jesus name might be denying the Trinity and as such they waited almost a full year to actually be baptized on April 15, 1914. This is going to produce a tremendous conflict as multitudes come forward to be baptized in Jesus name and it threatens much of the establishment. This conflict is ongoing, and like Ewart and Cook, it has not been resolved with the Persian evangelist. He, as many in the Pentecostal movement is in turmoil. At just about the time Ewart is baptized and conflict is starting, A.D. Urshan will go to Iran. This is an unresolved issue and has been put on the back burner because of all the turmoil both bad and good that he has been experiencing.

It seems that believers in Russia are themselves in turmoil about what to do with the Jesus name, one God message. Now is this because in private conversation he has shared the conflict with them? In their testimonies they comment that they had heard about this in America. Well, communication was opened between the East and West, and America, Britain and Russia were strong allies, so it is possible that through periodicals, or one person telling another it had already reached Petrograd even before he'd arrived. Russia was hurting at this moment, and everyone's lives were unstable and there was great deprivation. Huge sums of money had been expended to build the trans-Siberian Railway. Unlike the United States which had left this primarily as a capitalistic venture, the Czar had stripped the nation's coffers to build this important rail system. Possibly they could've recovered, but because of the

Germans they have had to go to war. In 1914 the Russians had been quite successful, but in 1915 the Germans had pushed back and had taken some key cities under the Russian protection. The war was going badly, and revolution was in the air. To add to all this, Rasputin was manipulating behind the scenes.

In general, evangelical preachers that believed in immersion were harassed, and there was a conspiracy that they were agents of the Germans trying to undermine the Czar. It was a state church situation to which we Americans are not accustomed, but the laws favored the Russian Orthodox Church, and there had been great persecution.

It may be hard for a present-day Apostolic to understand the mindset of the early pioneers, who like the Christians in Jerusalem at the very beginning, could not conceive of the idea of not being a part of the religious group with which they had always been involved. To the New Testament Jewish Christian in the early chapters of the book, Acts of the Apostles, a Christian would've considered himself simply a part of the Jewish community. To A. D. Urshan, Haywood and others they would simply have felt they were part of the evangelical movement and not separate; but within it sharing about how they had received the Holy Ghost speaking in tongues. They assumed that anyone that believed the word of God would want to know this and experience it. It was not connected in their mind with being part of a salvation message. They are enthusiastic and eager to share it.

When they came to water baptism, this seemed to be an issue of truth, but had little significance other than on the matter of it being truth. Because of this they are all moving rather slowly. They do not want to cause controversy; they are rather centrist evangelicals and fundamentalists. The idea of denying the Trinity is, on the surface, repugnant to them. It is important to understand for both The Apostolic Pentecostals and the Trinitarian Pentecostals that they could not envision the idea receiving the Holy Ghost with the sign of speaking in tongues as causing a controversy. When it happened to most of them they eagerly went back to tell their congregations about what had happened and when they did, they did not find the warm reception they were expecting. This was to them a not "must-have issue," but rather "you can have it proclamation."

Therefore, the subject of being baptized with the name Jesus invoked over you was of very little significance other than simply being truth. When confronted with the idea that to speak the name Jesus at baptism was a denial of the Trinity; it caused Ewart and Cook to stop completely for one year. It caused A. D. Urshan, who had been baptizing in Jesus name from a much earlier period, to stop baptizing when asked to do so by Pioneers Durham and Ewart. These would each be asking for different reasons as Ewart asked for it to study the matter and not cause controversy; and Durham did not want the controversy. Because of this, he had gone to baptizing in the name of the Father, Son and Holy Ghost.

This Persian Evangelist had been invited to Vyborg by the Free Protestant Mission to minister in their churches, but he will quickly meet with Pastor Ivanov and be invited to preach at the Christian Evangelical Church. This would mean that the beliefs must have been similar. The Christian Evangelical Church grows out of the Anabaptist tradition and is generally called Baptist there. The point I'm making is that Anabaptist, called Baptist in Europe, are not to be confused with the Baptist churches or the Southern Baptist Convention that exists in the United States. The thought process between these two groups is quite different.

What will take place now by Providence is a sovereign work of the Holy Ghost, and the controversy over the idea of baptism invoking the name of Jesus is causing interest. Now let's add to this that the real controversy that remains to this day both in Europe and here in the United States is the issue of, what they would term, "rebaptized." In Russia, and out of the history of Poland, there had already been introduced some notion of baptizing in Jesus name according to Acts 2:38 as being true, but also, many believed Matthew 28:19 to be saying that people were to be baptized with the use of the words," Father, Son and Holy Ghost." In other words, they would say that you could baptize either way. The issue was that once you were baptized, this was a settled work, and that to be rebaptized was calling into question that one of the ways is incorrect. In fact, among the Russians some would argue that to be baptized in the Russian Orthodox Church, even as a baby was enough, and that you should not be rebaptized. This idea of rebaptism was an incredibly radical and disturbing idea to the Russian mind. It would take God to cause this to happen.

Even though on a personal level everything that A. D. Urshan understood caused him to think that no one needed rebaptized, yet he knew this wasn't truth and he was in turmoil. This turmoil became so great that it shut down his ministry for a very brief period, as he said, "he could do nothing." He prayed and sought God and continued to struggle with this. He realized there were many passages concerning baptism in Jesus' day, and finally in desperation he cried out to the Lord asking if this is the right way then please have someone come to me and ask to be baptized this way and have them point to the Scripture that says this is the right way to be baptized.

Let me quote from his own testimony as preserved in **The Chronicle** by the Russians,

> "Very soon we received God's revelation and were convinced that He was revealing the Truth" This was my prayer: "Lord, if you command me to baptize those converted in this meeting in the name of Jesus Christ, as it said in Acts 2:38, 8:16, 10:48, 19:5, let someone ask me to do so, without my suggestion or asking it. Make that person show me the Bible verse telling of water baptism in the name of Jesus Christ." I promised God that if he gave me the sign of His Will, I would not hesitate to perform the baptism. Before I tell you the result of my prayer, please consider

that none of the Russians knew what was happening in America at the time. Despite that fact, much to my surprise, one night at a meeting when God's power was upon us, a big man rose up from the congregation hurried down the aisle with a Bible in his hand. He'd been converted a few meetings back. Tears were running down his face; he was holding the Bible with a finger stuck in it on the page we all needed to read. He cried: "Brother Urshan! The Lord Jesus Christ told me last night to ask you to baptize me exactly the way it is written here." It was Acts 8:16. I said nothing, only silently thanked the Lord. At the next meeting I said I intended to conduct water baptism in the name of Jesus Christ. I asked everyone to pray to find a right place where I can baptize that man and all others who wish to be baptized."

This is now no longer an issue with Andrew David Urshan. It is now a matter of conscience. It is God speaking to him and telling him that he must baptize this new way, which is really the original way. It's not a matter of doctrinal debate, or something he wants to do. By doing this he realizes there are many things he will lose. As it is, he has great standing with pushed out and pushed aside people, and he is well aware of what that means. For him to baptize and be baptized in Jesus name will separate him; not because this is what he wants, but he realizes there is a controversy and the division. This is not an easy matter of flesh, but easy because God is giving him directions.

This baptism is an extremely important event in Russian history; because it is not only the introduction of the message, but the foundation of the Christian Evangelical Church in the Spirit of the Apostle's founding. There has already been somewhat of a brotherhood established between Ivanov and Smorodin, with Ivanov pastoring a nice church in Vyborg, and now the good congregation is being established in Petrograd that Smorodin will pastor. These men had all been together at the development of God giving the importance of this message, but two things were still needed: Urshan himself to be baptized in Jesus name, and Smorodin's wife to accept this for the church to really go forward.

Maria Aleksandovana Smorodina was from a very prominent Russian family, and almost Royal herself. Her mother had served in the house of Prince Obolensky. To Americans this may not seem like much, but in this imperial world such a position was incredibly important. Even today I have seen this name associated in Washington DC with foundations such as the Russian House. This is important because this was a significant Russian family, and very honorable. Her father was very wealthy, and all the children had private tutors that taught them.

She had struggled with converting to be an evangelical and this had been a hard process, but now the idea of being rebaptized, as she considered it, was simply absurd. She loved her husband but was not prepared to follow him in this matter and therefore God himself would have to talk to her. In the same manner Urshan had resolved to return to the United States to be baptized.

I realize that the translation quotes from Russian to English have many errors but have left them, so the flavor of these quotes remains.

Her testimony as preserved in the **Chronicle** reads as follows:

"I went to Petrograd to attend a meeting of an Estonian congregation of which I had learned from my husband's postcard; he had visited those meetings and told me they were very lively. I went to the place where Russian Christian Evangelicals gathered together. At the time the meetings were frequented by Rev. Urshan. He had gone to native Persia (Iran) was about to return to America. It was Easter. And Urshan was asked to baptize a few people. Before my arrival here he had already baptized in that meeting several persons in the name of the Father, Son, and the Holy Spirit. So, it was Easter time, and many wanted to be baptized. Snow had just melted; the day was warm. It was near The Black River outside Petrograd. When we arrived, the meeting was already in progress and Brother Urshan was preaching the word of God. In his sermon, he mentioned two other American brothers who shared his beliefs. He told the listeners how they a short while back and then praying together when they had a revelation about the place in the gospel where it said that one should be baptized in the name of the Father, Son, and Holy Spirit but in the name of Jesus Christ. Joined in these thoughts, the three of them decided they were going to be baptized in the way upon returning to America. He related all that to the meeting, revealing it to all listeners and those that had come to receive baptism. Urshan prayed and asked the Lord to allow him to be baptized in the name of Jesus Christ in America, as he and his friends had resolved. But he was told through the Holy Spirit: 'No, Andrew, you are going to receive baptism here.' Listening to his sermon then I thought to myself: Oh, if only God pointed to me the exact place in the Bible where it says that one must be baptized in the name of Jesus Christ, I would immediately receive such baptism." And just at that moment the Rev. Urshan started to read the passage where the Ephesians were baptized in the name of Jesus Christ (Acts 19:1 − 5). It became clear to me that it was necessary to be baptized in the name of Jesus Christ (before then, my husband and I have been baptized in the name of the Father, Son, and the Holy Spirit.) Many brothers had similar revelations, and they told Urshan that there were many among them who wanted to be baptized in the name of Jesus Christ. They had doubts about one thing: since Urshan had not been baptized in the name of Jesus Christ who was to perform the baptism? Finally, they decided to let the oldest member of the congregation, brother Antonov, baptize Urshan. Then Urshan baptized all others who wanted (men and women). Some were baptized for the first time, but others had previously been baptized in the name of the Father, Son and the Holy Spirit had the truth revealed to them at the meeting and were also baptized. It was then that my husband N. P. Smorodin and I received baptism."

"This is how the true teaching of the Lord Jesus Christ came to Russia. Several members of the Vyborg congregation, together with Smorodin and Ivanov formed the first commune of followers of the Apostolic Christian teaching in Petrograd in 1916."

All of this happened on the eve of Urshan's return to the United States. There are now several members, two churches, two pastors, and thus a fellowship organization.

Andrew David Urshan laid hands on Nikolai Smorodin and anointed him as the leader of the new group. There is a great deal of interest, and this church group will grow rapidly. It thinks of itself as an organization and in about a year and a half will file papers with the new communist government for recognition. These papers will be approved and signed by no less than Vladimir Lenin himself. This makes the work of Urshan special and different from other evangelists that have been preaching a Pentecostal message in Russian.

## DESCRIPTION OF APPLICANT.

Age: *31* years.
Stature: *5* feet, *10½* inches, Eng.
Forehead: *broad*
Eyes: *black*
Nose: *long*

Mouth: *small*
Chin: *pointed*
Hair: *black*
Complexion: *dark*
Face: *round*

## INDENTIFICATION.

*Tabriz, August 12, 1915*

I hereby certify that I know the above-named *Andrew D. Urshan*
personally, and know *him* to be the identical person referred to in the within-described
Certificate of Naturalization, and that the facts stated in h *is* affidavit are true to the best of
my knowledge and belief.

*Mihran Baghdasarian*

[Address of witness.] *Tabriz, Persia.*

Identifying documents submitted as follows: *Applicant registered at this
Consulate, October 1, 1914. His naturalization Certificate and U.S.
passport were stolen from his residence during the Turkish occupation
of Urumia in January 1915.*

NOTE.—This form is to be filled out in duplicate, one copy being retained in the files of the issuing office and the other
forwarded to the Department of State.

*The applicant desires an Emergency passport
for use in transit through Russia and such other
Countries as it may be necessary to pass in return-
ning as quickly as possible to his home in the
United States.*

*Gordon Paddock*

*Consul*

U - 6 2 5

Family name

Urshan

Given name or names

Andrew David

Address

821 N. Clark St., Chicago, Illinois

Certificate no. (or vol. and page)

F-984  Ch 276774

Title and location of court

J. S. Circuit

Country of birth or allegiance

Persia

When born (or age)

May 3, 1884

Date and port of arrival in U. S.

Aug. 15, 1902  New York

Date of naturalization

Dec. 13, 1904

Names and addresses of witnesses

George Tyson  Chicago Opera House  Block Chgo., Ill.

John A. Miguel  Yada Bldg., Chicago, Ill.

Andrew David Urshan was born in 1885 and raised in a Presbyterian family. His religious experience is varied depending on who is discussing it. Urshan always spoke of being saved when he was a Presbyterian, however according to him, he will now begin his return to the United States, on that return we know he stopped at Oslo, Norway and met with a prominent minister by the name of Barrett. He will sail from Bergen to Newcastle, England and spend a period of time in England with the Boddys. He will hold services with them preaching and from Liverpool, he will depart in July 1960, arriving back home in New York.

Brother and Sister Andrew D. Urshan's Wedding Picture

Andrew David Urshan, back in the United States will have things happen very rapidly for him in that he will shortly thereafter marry and begin his family. He will begin preaching the Jesus name message in the North, around Wisconsin, Michigan and Indiana. He will write a book and he will become a pioneer in the development of the Jesus name church organizations in the United States and Canada. His driving burden will be for missions and he will become a missionary director for the Pentecostal Assemblies of the World. He will join with others in forming a variety of apostolic groups, some of which will later be the United Pentecostal Church.

Family will be his great blessing and tragic sorrow. His wife will leave him, and he will maintain the custody of all the children and raise them on a preacher's salary. Each of the family members will have a unique sweetness to them as the result of their father.

For all of us, our happiest times and our saddest times generally revolve around family. Even in the most perfect setting, that is a young man and a young woman meet, marry, have children, raise them and enjoy life together for 60 or 70 years: It is blissful, and this will be their happiest times. The day comes when one dies, and it is their saddest day. For him, he married and had children and as they were growing, his wife left him. Now, if this is not enough sadness, some to whom he ministered and preached together, and with whom he had been friends turned against him. He's devastated, and he is at his lowest peak. At this point, he retreats for a brief period to South Bend, Indiana. Here he will find comfort as Bishop Rowe will minister to him. He will tell Bishop Rowe that if it had not been for him he could very easily have lost everything. He will be rejuvenated and go back preaching the gospel and raise his children. Later, he will marry a woman with children by the name of Dugas and together these wonderful people will raise a number of children to become pastors and pastor's wives and will influence the Apostolic Movement.

Out of his great suffering will grow that beautiful song "There Is Sunshine in the Shadows." When you listen to the song you can catch a glance of the intense suffering that this man went through. There is a great lesson for young ministers to learn from the lives of Andrew David Urshan and Nathaniel A. Urshan. Both are driven to preach the gospel, both are outstanding, both will stay with the church and will have recognition. One will suffer far more than the other with the younger gathering far more recognition. When you stand back and examine the difference between the two it will be the women they married.

If you listen carefully you can sense the tremendous pain he went through at this time of trial. Read the words of his song. Words and music by Andrew David Urshan:


"The Sunshine in the Shadow"

When life is burdened with sorrow,

And it seems all help is gone,

Jesus whispers "do not falter;

I will leave thee not alone."

Then somehow amidst my trials,

how it is I cannot see;

Still I hear a voice from heaven,

Gently saying, "follow me."

Sometimes my friends do forsake me,

And I'm tempted to despair;

Then I think of my dear Jesus – to lay his head he had nowhere.

Oh, it pays to follow Jesus,

Just to learn from him each day;

And I guarantee, my brother,

You'll have sunshine all the way.

Let me recommend him to you;

I have found no friend like Him,

he is One who will never deceive you,

But stay with you to the end.

If you would have peace and comfort,

Let his banner be unfurled.

He was lifted up on Calvary,

And his name can save the world

Chorus

There is sunshine in the shadow;

There is sunshine in the rain;

There is sunshine in our sorrow,

When our hearts are filled with pain.

There is sunshine when we're burdened;

There is sunshine when we pray;

There is sunshine, Heavenly sunshine,

Blessed sunshine all the way.


Brother Urshan in the United States was a little out of step with people here. There was an intensity about him, and extreme passion for the gospel. In Russia it is common for evangelicals when they eat dinner to stand, perhaps read a Scripture, sing a song and all join in prayer. They will even do this when they are dining out in the restaurant. This was somewhat the norm for him, but the rest of the group here in the United States could find it uncomfortable. I remember as a child Brother Hugh Rose complaining that he had to take A. D. Urshan to lunch and he knew what was going to take place. A. D. Urshan when entering a house would follow the Biblical admonition and would say "Peace unto this house." He would often tell his son, "I do not feel enough prayer here."

Until the day he died, he would travel and preach in churches, small and great. When he was younger he had his "rolling Bible school." He had charts and would teach Genesis to Revelations. He did not distinguish between church organizations but would preach outside the United Pentecostal Church in churches that were Bread of Life, and a variety of organizations. He did not let organization hinder him or get in the way; he was building the kingdom of God.

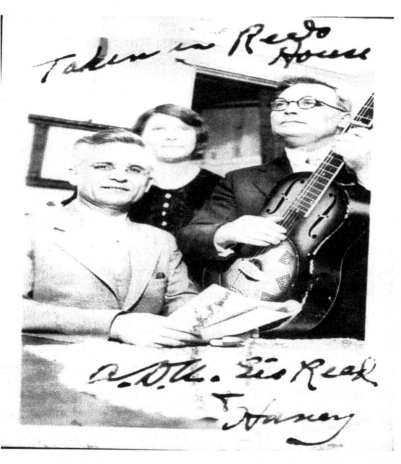

When I was very young, perhaps 14 or 15 years of age, he came to Calvary Tabernacle, my home church, to preach and I was listening intently, as his accent was very thick.

Now, Calvary Tabernacle is designed in such a way that there is a large prayer room behind the platform area with doors on either side for you to go into the back. Seldom is the altar call ever upfront, but instead as the altar call is given, people will stream through the doors back into the prayer room to pray. Two events shaped my life at Calvary Tabernacle and they were both at the front of the church and not in the prayer room. One of these was on this occasion that he was preaching and when he concluded he said, "I'm going to lay hands on all those that wish to have hands laid on them. " A line was formed of everyone wanting to be prayed for by him. I was one of those that was not extremely serious but rather was a "go with the flow guy." As he prayed for people for some he gave, what would be considered, a prophetic utterance or a word of knowledge. When he came to me, or rather as I passed between both Brother Urshan and his son, he laid hands on me and prophesied I would be a minister. To this day in remembrance, I feel that he was anointing me for the work I would do in Russia. I believe that this was God's anointing and that likely at that moment, neither he nor I realized the implication.

At any rate, he had a profound influence on my life. As I was growing up, teachers in the school at Calvary Christian School would share with us letters Brother Urshan had received and they would talk about them. I can specifically remember on one occasion when likely, Sister Miller, was sharing about people in the country of Russia writing to him and asking for money to buy a cow. They felt that the government was forcing them to do this and would then simply take the money, as he had tried to help in the past and it had come to nothing. I grew up hearing of his revivals in that part of the world, and more importantly seeing him and hearing.

To many of us, he is a Pentecostal pioneer, a deeply spiritual man, and an awesome figure. Bishop Samuel Smith, The General Chairman and Presiding Bishop of the Apostolic World Christian Fellowship, related to me how in 1964, when he was attending Apostolic Bible Institute, he was sent to meet A. D. Urshan. He was a senior at school and had a very nice car as he worked to support himself through school, so he had been selected for this honor. He went to the airport close to St. Paul in his 1957 Chevy to bring this great pioneer of the faith to the school. He remembers how tense he was feeling as though he was carrying God Himself in the car. He asked the question, "What advice can you give me for my ministry?" Brother Urshan said, "S-A-M-U-E-L, you must have a passion for souls". I'm not saying compassion as that causes you to feel sorry for them. I am saying, a passion. You must want it as the drug addict wants drugs, as the alcoholic wants alcohol. It must drive you and you must be desperate for it." Bishop Smith relates how that moment was a driving force for his ministry.

To many he was this awesome figure, but there is his family and to them he was daddy and grandpa. Pastor James Larson posted on Facebook a comment about his grandfather that I found gave insight to the warmth of his personality. I asked if I might use it in this book with his

110

permission, and was granted, and I am sharing with mild editing.

"In the 1950s, in St. Paul, Minnesota, a 57 Chevy loaded with kids on a cold winter's day pulled up to the train station, frosty windows had breath fogging up the viewing. My kindergarten mind trying to have understanding as he emerged, white headed, short stature, and a full length, navy black wool coat and a scarf, always dashing. My Grandpa Andrew David Urshan, he would squeeze my cold cheeks and kiss my mouth. "In Jesus name" bless my Jimmy, he said in broken English. I had no idea of his significance, as he had pastored, Midway Tabernacle after G.T. Haywood, and before S.G. Norris in St. Paul. A real survivor of the Assyrian massacre, this man had witnessed to Muslims who had murdered the innocent, cutting off heads of Christians and with women stabbing them with swords in the abdomen. At home now, he would take over! Set me on the piano, and he would sing in Aramaic (What he called the Jesus language). In English he would sing, There Is Sunshine in the Shadow! If not this, another song he had written. Cooking us Middle Eastern food – I could never forget the aromas and the love! His prayer time was in the early hours of the morning and it has never left my mind. Laying hands on my head, he would pray for God to use me and to bless me. So, 55 years later I'm still impacted by his prayers! We know that Jesus Christ is our help and Savior and his NAME is a strong tower!"

Red Square

# Chapter Four

## The Soviet Years

Andrew Urshan had departed Russia leaving them with a revelation of the name of Jesus and the power of the Holy Ghost. He had a church set in order with N. P. Smorodin as the leader of this church group. These were key men that were going to establish a significant work and be the dominant expression of the Pentecostal movement in that country for the early stage until the 1920s.

Nikolai P. Smorodin was to be the key leader. He was born in 1875 and was a native of the St. Petersburg region. Like many of the early Pentecostal Pioneers of this faith group, he would come out of the military and would have been a loyal czarist. He had leadership capabilities, and this could be seen in the fact that his government had made him the supervisor of a military hospital in Finland in a small force that was left behind after the Russo – Swedish War. There he would meet his faithful mate that would be with him through his life; they married in 1907. Maria Aleksandovana Shurigina was an ethnically and nationally Russian living in Finland, or properly, the Great Principality of Finland, Russian Empire.

His wife Maria, born in 1882, was from a prestigious family. Her mother served in the family of Prince Obolensky which was a noble family going back to the very foundation of the Kievian royalty. To an American, to say she was a servant in this household would make very little sense as a place of honor, but it was very prestigious at the time of the czars. Her father was a wealthy merchant and was able to employ private tutors to give them a quality education. All the children were literate at a time when this was not so common.

Nikolai and Maria were well-suited for each other and it was going to take this and all their strengths and brilliance to establish the Pentecostal message across Russia and to guide this new movement through the horrible Soviet Period.

In 1909, Nikolai Smorodin served for a brief time as a midshipman in the Baltic Fleet; it was staged most of the time in Abo. There he met a sailor by the name of Pagonov, who was an Evangelical Christian. In the Russian history, sailors often had a more open and enlightened view as they had encountered the West and other forms of society. It was noted that there were Russian sailors at the Azusa Street revival. This sailor had been sent to repair the heating system in the Somordin's apartment. This took several days, and during this time Paganov shared with Midshipman Nikolai, his faith. The spreading of Protestant or Evangelical teaching in the Army was against regulations as the Czar was loyal and faithful to the Russian Orthodox Church.

Over a period of time, Nikolai came to be quite close friends with Pagonov, but Maria with her strong czarist background was actually disturbed. Over time Maria began to warm and listen to what he was saying. Pagonov, was in fact, a minister and an evangelist among the Christian

Evangelical Churches. He had made a convert in these two and this was the beginning of their spiritual journey toward a more Bible centered teaching. With the shortage of ministers in that country, Smorodin quickly became an evangelist himself. The friends he made, Ivanov and Tuchov, soon began preaching a personal relationship with Jesus Christ and justification by faith. They preached all around the Gulf of Finland from Helsinki to St. Petersburg in villages and cities.

The Smorodins would next become associated with A. I. Ivanov and be active in his church that he pastored at Vyborg. Ivanov was part of a great evangelical revival that had established strong Evangelical Christian Churches in the area from Finland to St. Petersburg. These men would work together proclaiming the evangelical message around this region.

To an American, the word Russia is identical to the term Soviet Union. In fact, we might use the term Russia in three ways: the historical territory that would later become the land of Russia, the invasion of the Rus or Vikings that later would give name to the land of Russia under its development of the Imperial Czar, and finally Russia dominating the old Soviet Union to the point that many would think of the Old Soviet as Russia. These are in fact three very different things to be brought together in our minds as Russia. Again, to an American, the word Soviet has an incredibly negative tone, and when one hears it they automatically think of the tyranny of the Cold War. Surprisingly, it does not have that meaning to those that live there and to them it simply means a union or a society. People in the churches might be shocked to hear that the term "Soviet Brodsky" is simply the term of the church board. Soviet Brodski meaning loosely, Union of Brothers or Board of Brothers.

The Soviet Revolution started out rather benign and was little more than hungry people pleading for food. The Russian Revolution might be more clearly defined as a series of revolutions with the first being in 1905. The heavy authoritarian hand of the state under the czar, the constant demand for money for such projects as the trans-Siberian Railway, and serfdom itself constantly eroded away the wealth of even the nobility to the point that there was once a study made and showed there was no prosperous area in all of Russia. The people demanding a share in the government sparked a revolution in 1905 that gave a shared government between the peoples elected, Duma and the Czar. This was an incredibly turbulent and troublesome time with the new weak government unable to provide needed resources for the country. This weak government often functioned through local Soviets of the people. This period had nothing to do with the Communist Party directly, and Vladimir Lenin was outside of the country. This weak and unstable government was going to eventually give rise to a communist takeover that would be known as the October Revolution of 1917 by the Bolsheviks. The Bolsheviks is a term meaning the majority, and ironically there was never a point where they ever had that majority.

In a well thought out plan, the Germans in an effort to win World War I and hoping to do so by getting Russia out of the conflict so that they would only have to fight on one front, orchestrated sending Vladimir Lenin with $10 million to Petrograd with the intention of his developing a revolution and that new government withdrawing from World War I, and it worked. Vladimir Lenin was systematically able to gain control of the various Soviets and eventually the overall government with his Bolsheviks. His first official act was to withdraw Russia from the conflict. Nevertheless, things remain in turmoil with ongoing fighting in the country between those loyal to the czar and the Bolsheviks.

To complicate matters, this is exacerbated by great shortages of foods and supplies because of the start of World War I. Among those suffering the greatest shortages of foods and supplies will be the Army itself that is being asked to risk its life with many dying. This was an unpopular war. The Czar and his family were being heavily questioned in the minds of the people due to their yielding so much influence on a semi-crazed minister by the name of Rasputin.

It is in this time of chaos that Andrew David Urshan has entered and began preaching in this Petrograd region. The instability can be seen in the changing of the name from St. Petersburg to Petrograd, and this is being done because the word burg sounds to German with whom the Russians are at war. Hundreds of years of tradition quickly laid aside for a new name. In the lives of the general population there was great concern and uncertainty, and this was especially felt in the area around Petrograd and Finland

It is surprising that Andrew Urshan accomplished so much in such a short time. He was in Russia a matter of months and even shorter in time is the time he spent in Petrograd, but he left with a congregation established. Vyborg had been the strong work in the past and it was a well-organized church but did not move forward with Jesus name message until after Urshan left. There remains a large church in St. Petersburg pastored today by Dmitry Shatrov. When I was there last, he showed me in the foyer pictures of all the pastors of the church and it started with Andrew David Urshan. He is the one that brought the message of the Holy Ghost, Jesus name and preached the revival that later would produce this great church in Petrograd.

I cannot state often enough the very fact and importance that what this man did was not just preach the gospel in the truth, but he established an organization. He set the church in order and placed Smorodin at the head of it. Now, Smorodin was assisted by some rather able men such as Ivanov, Rudolph Nolte, and many others. There are names in their history to which we are unaccustomed such as Boris Rud'ko, Andrei Goryachin, Vasily Kalegin, Nickolai Shishkov, Averkiev and Piotr Gramovich. These are all names that we need to study and learn more about, and no doubt a book could be written about each of these men. One name that will be of great significance later in their history is Shatrov and his entire family. These are men that will develop the Apostolic Church called the Christian Fvangelical Church in the Spirit of the Apostles and will dominate the Russian scene for Pentecostalism for almost 20 years and will bring it through the time of the Soviet oppression.

Ivanov which has been such a close friend with Smorodin deserves a little attention at this point. He was described as "well-educated" and was greatly respected among those of the evangelical faith in the Gulf of Finland Region. At first, he rejected the Jesus name message which he described as "strange and incomprehensible." He seems to have resented and disliked Urshan, or at least was jealous of his ministry. Ivanov could not understand the influence that A. D. Urshan was gaining in his region when he had to speak through a translator, and he says of Urshan "Was not very convincing even then." Here is Ivanov, a successor to the prominent and famous I. S. Prokhanov and is well educated and articulate and yet the demonstration of power at Urshan's meetings are drawing the people and convincing them, when Ivanov, is not able to hold people to his point of view. He knows Urshan is leaving for America soon and he is really looking forward to this. He witnessed the demonstration of the moving of the Holy Ghost and miracles and knew that God was with the Persian Evangelist, especially at one meeting in the Serdolbolsk district near Vyborg.

Shortly after Urshan leaves for which we have no exact date but must've still have been in 1916, Ivanov accepts baptism in Jesus name by Smorodin. This is significant because it is the conversion of a major Christian Evangelical pastor. The things that were strange to this man's ears was not just the Jesus name message, but also the Holy Ghost speaking in tongues. This would've been like the pastor of First Baptist Church in your town receiving the Holy Ghost and being baptized in Jesus name. This gave the movement a big church in that region, and another significant leader.

In 1918, Smorodin and Ivanov wrote a letter to the head of the new communist government Vladimir Lenin asking for legal status to open, what the Russians term, "A Praying House" and what we would call a church building, in Petrograd. This was granted and to this day the Apostolic Church in Russia points with pride to the early validation of their church group giving them legal status even in this present Russian government. Because of it they are not considered a "New Religion." The People's Commissar for Enlightenment, A.V. Luncharsky determine there was nothing wrong with this group's teaching and that perhaps it should be studied.

The official legalization of the church did not mean that it would be without persecution. At the beginning of the revolution there was a certain excitement about the defeat of the Czar and a hope for religious freedom. This had taken shape in two forms, first, when the Duma was permitted with the Czar to begin to make some laws in a minor democratic fashion and when this was done religious freedom was written into the law but not really granted, and second with the defeat of the Czar the Bolsheviks again promised religious freedom. A. D. Urshan in his book says towards the end of last year there was a revolution in Russia and now there would be religious freedom. He was looking forward to the soon return of himself to Russia.

In theory religious freedom and the legalization of the church was given on paper, but as our brothers in Russia record in their book, The Chronicles, "not all that was legal was permitted." The persecution came in waves with the first being in Lenin's time. The heaviest persecution would come under Stalin, with a brief time of tolerance from World War II to Churchill's statement concerning the Iron Curtain, then heavy persecution again, and slightly less persecution under Gorbachev and Brezhnev. Smorodin would be arrested so many times even his closest followers would have a hard time keeping track of how often. He died in prison and was buried in an unmarked grave.

Through it all, these humble followers of Christ would take pride in the fact that they were Russian and do everything they could to cooperate with the government. Pastor P. N. Koloskov, Of the Apostolic Praying House in Moscow, was one that Vladimir Lenin would often turn to for help in meeting the social needs in the early struggling days of his government. He asked the church to help with orphans and feeding of the homeless and their needs. Because of these faith-based social programs, Lenin protected the church in Moscow. People began calling these social workers, the sober ones, because they preached to the people that they should stay away from alcohol, crime and begging. Despite this working together early on, soon this pastor was arrested and sent to the gulags. The social programs were disbanded, and Stalin would outlaw them altogether later.

It would be hard for us in the United States to imagine atheism as a formal religion. I might point out that while it is difficult to imagine, it is preached under the guise of secular humanism in our public schools quite often now. Russia has always been a church state government with an official church or religion. This was no different in the time of the Soviets when atheism became the official religion of the state. Vladimir Lenin and his closest allies would introduce scientific militant atheism in every aspect of the society with propaganda workers being sent out to the most remote rural areas of the Soviet. The local bosses of the Soviets had held back in the beginning but were only waiting for a signal from Moscow to begin persecution. It is no accident that E. Yaroslavtev would name his organization the Union of Militant Atheists. You would soon see in most major cities The Museum of Atheism and Other Religions. By 1932 there would be 10 anti-religious daily newspapers and 23 atheistic monthly magazines in the Soviet, this even though the USSR Constitution forbade forceful eradication of individual faith.

The persecution was intense and included even small things such as: the refusal of renting property including homes to individuals that were Christian, the withholding of their paychecks, and the barring of their going to school. One thing that was very meaningful to these humble Christian believers was the issue of motherhood and this with large families. The Soviet awarded medals, such as the Medal of

Motherhood, The Order of Hero Mother, and the Order of Mother's Glory. This was usually connected with the number of children to which a mother gave birth. The government in their persecution often would not issue these medals to these women, and even worse would give the medal and then come back later to take it away. Such small things might seem almost laughable to an American, but it hurt these poor souls deeply.

One had to study atheism at every level of education. One ironic thing that happened was that the Commissar for Religious Enlightenment published *A Bible for Believers and Nonbelievers.* It became popular in the churches because while it was printed to make fun of religious verses and finding fault, believers that had been forbidden to have Bibles, (Bibles had been outlawed), were able to read small portions of Scripture.

The persecution was beyond anything most of us could imagine. The gulags were not just the prison but rather a place you were expected to slowly die. Tens of thousands would be rounded up, selected, and sent off to these death camps in which 90% would die the first year. You would be put in cattle cars on a train taken out into Siberia and there you would begin a long march into a land that would be frozen and desolate in the winter and swampy quagmire in the summer. When the prisoner arrived, there were only a few buildings, perhaps a place for the camp commandant and his family to live, and some buildings for the guards. You would be told to get busy building some form of shelter in which to live.

Such places did not originate with the communist and had been long used in Russia since the time of the czars. You can hear it referred to in such popular works as *Fiddler on the Roof.* One of the shocking things of these places is that despite this hardship, wives not sent to prison with their husbands would find their way to the camp to join her husband. This is how towns and churches began in the interior of Russia. It is true that the persecution was far more general and heartless in the time of the Soviet. People were sent there for simply having faith in Christ and as such disturbing the atheistic model. Educated people which the Communists hated because of their intelligence were sent, as well as political dissenters, and just ordinary people's names that had been put on the list by Stalin or someone else.

To give some idea of the horrible persecution of this time let us take the testimony of a brother in Christ, an apostolic believer that did nothing more than simply possess a Bible which had been outlawed. G.M. Golokov was arrested in 1936 for having a Bible. Interestingly to us as Americans with all our values of our rights papers and security a search was made for the Bible, but he had hidden it so well it could not be found. This fact did not set him free but only made the authorities angrier and he was sentenced to the terrible Solovki Special Purpose Camp which would become in fact the model of the Soviet gulags. Alexander Solzhenitsyn describes it as the mother of gulags. It was designed to test how much the human spirit could endure through deprivation and persecution. It was here the NKVD was refined and developed. This prison was on a small island in the White Sea and this idea of islands may have given rise to the term Gulag. Our dear brother Golikov would spend 10 years in this horrible place because he was suspected of having a Bible.

The prison camps in Siberia were no better where the daily food ration was 300 g of brand that you could heat on a shovel over an open fire with mud water to make a cake each day. Prisoners poorly clothed and fed soon got scurvy and typhus and tuberculosis. The guards took delight in punishing people by depriving them of food, stripping them of clothing and tying them to a post where the mosquitoes would torment them. A sweet Sister of the Apostolic Faith was sent to such a prison in 1937, and her name was E. I. Koroleva for her faith in God. Her first year in prison at the NKVD where of the 50,000 prisoners brought in only 5000 remained after the first year. Later she would testify that she saw people frozen to death while cutting timber. During the second year of the camp the commandant discovered that she was a good seamstress and he spared her from the woodcutting assignment and was sent to the camps tailor shop where her talents blossomed. In 1947 she was released for a brief period and rearrested in 1949 having had a couple of years to visit with people from the church and share with them that she was still strong in the faith and living for God. On her second arrest she was sentenced to exile for life to Kazakhstan. After various appeals she was finally granted a pardon in 1956. Her body wracked, toothless and aged but testifying that God had kept her through it all and lived to the age of 93.

These wonderful saints whose names we should learn and remember, were heroes of faith of which the world was not worthy, and one day will stand with Jesus Christ to judge all men.

Ivan Kissel was arrested and sent to prison for about 30 years for simply having in his possession a Bible. Believers were classified as the worst category of prisoner, equivalent to be a traitor to your nation and an agent working against your government. They were sent to the worst possible gulags. Kissel was arrested in the 1930s and was not released until 1953. His was a large family with six brothers and one time there was a point in which all six brothers were in prison for being Christian. He was finally released during the time when the Soviets were easing persecution under Khrushchev. The Kissel family continues to minister in Maykop and have built a beautiful praying house on the main road of this city declaring the apostolic truth.

It can be said that persecution of believers has always existed and that would include present-day. We might consider some of the things they go through unbearable because of our tremendous religious freedom, but they were so used to heavy persecution that when the persecution was light it was a time of great joy. I can even see how God's hand was at work through Providence permitting certain things to happen that provided an environment for the start and development of the church.

In considering some of the things that God seemed to have orchestrated, let's look first at the fact that God brought A.

D. Urshan from the south of Russia to the north of Russia and to St. Petersburg. This was a prime location as there was greater tolerance there; and also, there was greater stability, food, and churches for the spread of this truth. While there were shortages in every part of the nation of the Soviet Union things were better in Petrograd, later Leningrad, than in the other parts of Russia. This gave a good base from which to minister and was providential that God had brought him to this area.

There were periods in which the communist exercised less persecution. In general, the years of Lenin were easier than the years of Stalin. After Stalin things became progressively better for the churches. There was something unusual that happened right at the very beginning of the Soviet Union that would provide a time that would hold persecution back for a brief period. In 1920 there was the Great Soviet Famine in which hundreds of thousands would die instead of the millions that were projected, because of the help brought by the American Relief Agency. World War I had been hard on all of Europe and Herbert Hoover, The Great Humanitarian, with his brilliant organizational skills had helped across Europe with relief mostly from America. Soviet Union was more complex with Russia having been our Ally in World War I but having turned. There was this new communist government in which most capitalist nations were very suspicious and did not trust. Hoover himself considered this nation to be a great evil.

Hoover did not want to propagate communism but as a humanitarian felt for the millions of innocent people that would die without food being sent. The story of the American Relief Agency would make a book in itself. Immediately shiploads of grain were brought together to be distributed all across Russia, and the focal point of that delivery would be Leningrad. This meant that there was more food there, and that things would be better in this area than any other. It also meant that the new Soviet government did not want to disrupt the help coming in from mostly the United States, and therefore would permit greater human rights for a brief period which gave the new church group a chance to get started before the persecution would hit. The United States required that they distribute seed grain across the country in 1921 that was not for eating, but only for planting. This gave them a good crop the next year and the famine was short-lived.

Extreme persecution would really get underway in the 1930s.There would be a second Great Famine in 1931 with most of it focused in the Ukraine. The Great Soviet Famine of 1920 was a combination of extreme bad weather coupled with poor socialistic policies, but the 1931 famine was in fact, a mean-spirited, intentional plan to kill millions in the Ukraine. Moscow, unlike the Americans, stripped the Ukrainians of their seeds for the next year. All Soviet Union was suffering under the heavy hand of communist leadership in the Soviet Union in the 30's.

The songs that were sung, and the poems written reflects some of the suffering of that time.

My friends, such was our lot,

Such it was for ages.

They tried to crush us with prison walls

In the lawless times of the czars.

Our brothers were in chains

In cold, far away northern lands.

All of Siberia was measured

By the tired feet of Christ's witnesses.

Threatening laws were written against us,

They tried to wipe us off the face of the earth.

But so was Christ persecuted in His time,

and Christians are alive up to this day.

Many of them fell on the battlefield

Far away from their loved ones.

Did they not die so that we might be awake?

A Russian Apostolic that had preserved in written documents from the earliest days of the revival speaks of the following song being a favorite of Christian prisoners from a hymn 49 from the book,

## The Songs of the First Christians.

People strictly forbid us

To preach of the cross

But we will listen to God

Rather than to people.


There are noisy crowds, everywhere is danger,

They are preparing chains for us

But we will listen to God

Rather than to people.

Near our meeting place

We see a watch of "guards"

But we will listen to God

Rather than to people.


And when they were hauled off to prison for long periods of time, one cannot imagine how difficult this was for family life. Russian Apostolic and other Christians traditionally had huge families with 15 or 16 children (eight children would not be a particularly large family.) Picture now a woman with several children and little or no means of support trying to keep the family together, feed them, and tell them of the love of God. You can begin to reflect the pain of the children being raised in this condition. One song speaks to me of this suffering.

Hello dear Dad!

Your beloved Sagas writing to you.

I miss you... They have separated us.

I'm waiting for you to come home.


Without you it is hard for our mom,

without you it is darker at night,

Winter is cold or without you…

Why did they accept prisons?


When I grow up I'll need the evil people

Take dads away from their kids,

And I will tell them in front of everyone:

"It is a sin to put a Christian on trial!"

Son can get used to being away from father.

And he can't understand

Why his father has been arrested and imprisoned

For God's testimony.

What is marvelous is the tremendous faith manifested by these believers in such difficult times. There was a positive message that grew out of this negative experience that is reflected in a very simple song.

Many hardships have we suffered.

Yet in our cloudy childhood

There were also right days

For when I was a child I met Christ.

Mothers did their best to keep the family together and to instruct the children in the ways of the Lord in a time and a society that was teaching them just the opposite. You can hear it in this song.

If they tell you:

"There is no God,"

You, children, must never believe

their words.

And the world of the proud ones,

Keep your heart, my son,

More than any precious thing.

There is no telling how many children did lose their faith to the constant, bombardment of the militant atheists. For example, Gagarin-- the first Russian cosmonaut, his wife was the daughter of a strong apostolic believer that seems to have been lost to the system. In our world we have our heroes, and in the East, they have theirs. This cosmonaut denied the existence of God and was one of their greatest heroes that brushed ever so closely with the truth of God's word (sort of the equivalent of Elvis and our society.)

Despite the persecution and deprivation, the churches flourished, grew, and expanded to other regions. The apostolic movement dominated in Russia until the 1930s when it came to Pentecostalism. Men such as, Nikita Demchuck, carried this message into Belorussia and Poland. A young man in the Army, Nikita met Somordin in 1916 and when he returned home established a youth group which would later grow into a church. Without a building or any resources, this young man would meet and pray in a rye field. It was believers such as this that carry the gospel everywhere. Ivanov reflecting later in a sermon said," We live in times when the Lord is trying everyone." We would all like to live together, but Satan scatters us believers like when they scatter seeds. Let us prepare ourselves and reinforce our faith. It is good to stay with the flock, but many will have to work their way to salvation alone." They did not seem to realize that, like the church in Jerusalem, God did not want them to stay together, but they would be seeds starting churches.

Smorodin carried on an exhausting schedule with the Holy Ghost guiding and providing. His children and wife rarely saw him as he was constantly traveling, preaching, or in jail. There are so many testimonies of his selflessness and the degree to which he was willing to go to serve the Lord. Hiking long distance through the snow to go and pray for a person that was sick, of which the Lord had spoken to him, and to see the person healed. It is hard for us to realize sitting here in America with all our ease and comfort how difficult the task was for this man. We get in our car and drive anywhere we want to go, stay in a Hotel, and have money and food. For him, if fortunate, it would be a long train ride, but in many cases, it was simply walking the roads often in the dead of winter with snow 3 feet or deeper.

Much later, in 1950 an incident occurred which demonstrated the Holy Ghost power of this man. One of the believers from Brest had been inducted in the service, and as a believer he was a conscientious objector and refused to carry a weapon or give the Communist pledge of no God and was to be court-martialed. The man had been tortured and persecuted by professionals, but still would not give in. Finally, he was to appear before the Colonel who began to interrogate him, and he finally asked, "What sect do you belong?" The young man replied he was Smorodin or Apostolic. The officer was shocked and asked, "Do you really believe as strongly as did Smorodin?" The officer asked, why didn't you say so at the beginning, you would've saved us a lot of time in torturing you as the officer was inferring he knew it would have been useless.

The Soviet officer had been at the trial of Smorodin. As was the custom, the prisoner could make a statement and once he began to speak, he spoke with such power and authority as the voice of God. The judge had tried to cut him off and was ordering him to stop, but the Russian officers loudly protested and said let him speak, let him have his say.

The officer explained that the conscientious objector was not dangerous. He said life will be hard for you here in the Army, but you will not be court-martialed. He was given very menial tasks to perform, but he was not sent to prison. You can imagine the power of this life of Smorodin that his words shook the very power of the Red Army, which was extremely powerful in 1950 so shortly after the war.

The church was growing and spreading. It was now about this time that another Russian comes home Ivan Efimovich Voronaev. This man was a Cossack under the Czar. Now this Russian word "Cossack" literally means "boots," and refers to mercenaries for hire. These were professional soldiers willing to work to the highest bidder and they were ruthless. He was converted in 1908 to be a Christian, of the evangelical type, which means his conversion had nothing to do with the Communist takeover as he had been a believer several years before that happened. He served as a Baptist pastor in Krasnoyarsk and Irkutsk. On one of my many adventures as a missionary, I traveled on the trans-Siberian Railway with Bishop Peter Rowe of South Bend, Indiana, and my Son-In-Law Greg Harris. Quite by happenstance, we met the pastor of the present-day Baptist Church, had dinner with him, visited the church, and heard the history of this group. This church was founded by four believers that were exiled to the city during the time of the Czar.

I want to emphasize again, that the whole of the Pentecostal revival church in Russia is homegrown or indigenous. Remember, Urshan was simply returning home. Smorodin and all the leaders were reputable Russians trying to live a good life in their society. Voronaev was a Russian born in Orenburg. While the Holy Ghost revival is universal and for all men everywhere, it is important for those in Russia to know that this was not some outside movement. He emigrated to the United States during time of extreme persecution launched by the state church against various sects, and this seems to be before the communist revolution. While this man is better known and is generally recognized as the major Pentecostal founder, we do not have as much information about him as we do, Urshan. This provides somewhat of an ironic twist, in a somewhat, rewriting of history to make the Christian Evangelical Church the more dominant. Sadly, both Pentecostals and Russians have lost so much of their history.

We know he comes first to San Francisco where the Baptists place him as pastor of a Russian Baptist Church. Three years later, he is invited to New York City, and while there converts to the Pentecostal movement. Keep in mind that Urshan had been in and out of New York City before and after this time. Did these two ever meet? This would be a very interesting question for which there seems to be no answer. Certainly, each man must have known about the work of the other. Voronaev will be remembered by many as the rather dominant leader.

German leader Gustav Herbert Schmidt born in Russia, and like Voronaev, became a Christian believer in 1908, and received the Holy Ghost speaking in tongues two or three years later. After finishing his degree in Germany immigrated to the United States where he attended the Rochester Bible Training School in New York, the Assembly of God appointed him a missionary to Poland in 1919 and he arrived there in 1920. Remember this is the time of the Great Soviet Famine, and with it, all of Europe is in a time depression following the end of World War I.

Schmidt will be involved in both preaching and humanitarian assistance, and this will cause the Pentecostal movement in his area of Poland to grow rapidly. All of this is important in dealing with Russia and the fact that from time to time, Poland will expand and contract in size and at this time is taken in the Ukraine. It is also important because much of Western Ukraine and parts of Poland are ethnically German and speak German.

In 1920 Voronaev has reached Bulgaria, which today is an apostolic Pentecostal stronghold, with their history telling of Russian sailors that started the work there and maybe those that were referred to at Azusa Street. He will come in and begin his work and will later join with Schmidt to begin preaching across much of the Ukraine. These men bring with them what the Apostolic Church is lacking, and that is money from America. These men as appointed missionaries will have much more money to work with, and Schmidt seems to have tapped humanitarian assistance being distributed across Europe. These men will form the Christian Evangelical Church – Pentecostal. Voronaev will be credited with founding 350 churches, most of them across the Ukraine; to give all this credit to this man, undermines both Schmidt and Urshan. He may have been more of a reorganizer and developer of existing churches.

Schmidt is a driving force that sees the need of Bible training centers for pastoral development. He petitioned the Assembly of God to start a Bible school and is turned down in 1925 because the AG feels overwhelmed with expenditures for mission work at this time. Providentially, wealthy men stepped up to underwrite his work, and on March 2, 1930 he starts the first Bible Training Center in Danzig. Now, the city which might be thought of as German was a semi-autonomous city that would be heavily German blood in Poland at that time. This work developed Poland into an extremely strong Assembly of God expression of the Pentecostal movement to this day. Very quickly Danzig becomes pro-Nazi and by 1938 Schmidt flees the country and comes to the United States.

Voronaev is arrested in 1929 and dies in prison. He leaves behind The Christian Evangelical Church – Pentecostal which remains the dominant Pentecostal expression in Russia to this day. As stated before, the bulk of it will be in the Ukraine, and of that mostly in western Ukraine. Because Western Ukraine was administered through Poland where they had greater freedom, and because of the work of Schmidt they sought and had Bible schools started as early as the 1960s.

It is interesting that the Christian Evangelical Church – Pentecostal has on its webpage the simplest expression of the existence of God. Let me quote a webpage of the Christian Evangelical Church Russia:

"We believe that five famous Protestant points:"

"We recognize God as the Supreme and Absolute Power."

"We recognize salvation as a free gift to all mankind

through Jesus' mercy and Grace given on the cross."

"We recognize the Holy Scripture as the only

source of Christian revival and right of each

Christian to understand and interpret the Bible."

"We recognize the church as 'Christian Fellowship' where the Gospel is preached in all its purity."

"We recognize the right of every Christian to pray to God without a 'so-called special mediator.'"

Now this is very interesting as the five famous Protestant points may be referring to five basic points of fundamentalism which does not correlate exactly with the Russian expression, and they seem not to be aware of this fact. The statement of the Christian Evangelical Church – Pentecostal will add two more points as we will discuss later. What is significant here is that this is also the expression of the Christian Evangelical Church in general which is usually termed Baptist. Hollenwager in his book, **The Pentecostals,** speaks to the fact that because of A. D. Urshan's early work, there is no statement on the Trinity among any of the Pentecostal nor Evangelical groups. I have little conflict here, because while this group identifies as Assembly of God there has been a real openness to Oneness of God and water baptism in Jesus name, and left to themselves it would never be an issue for the Russians as it is their history. Nevertheless, pressure is constantly put on them from America to adopt a more American view of the Assembly of God's position. And even pointing this out, I will be making it harder-while this is not my intent-it is still important to point out the work that Urshan accomplished.

It is said in Moscow even the Baptists baptized in Jesus name, and this became dominant early. Seemingly, Voronaev and Schmidt did not want to fight this battle, and thus organized a rather open statement of faith.

There is no statement of faith among The Christian Evangelicals – Pentecostals concerning the subject of water baptism. Members of this group that did not accept the apostolic message often urged me to work within it to start my own churches which they would happily accept that would be permitted to baptize no other way than in Jesus name. One pastor named Roman in Moscow told me that if I wanted he would argue my right to start churches in this group's name as their bylaws permitted this Jesus name message.

This will later cause confusion when dealing with a group called the Siberian Seven. If you ask a member of the Christian Evangelical Churches if they believe in baptism in Jesus name, they will always say yes, that's Bible. Many have been baptized in Jesus name as they baptized both ways. The difference between them and the Apostolic Church is that we call all to be baptized in Jesus name and that if baptized some other way they should be rebaptized.

To emphasize the fact that they downplay water baptism even though they're excited about it and will even break the ice to baptize you in the dead of winter, let us look at the last two points of their confession:

"We believe in the Apostolic baptism of the Holy Spirit with signs manifesting with spiritual gifts for His Church to be shaped, with believers being raised up to bring unbelievers to faith. We believe it biblical order that Apostles had confirmed for us, for premarital relations, for church structure, for worship and devotion."

"We believe in missions where we have to reach out to each tribe in every nation. We believe in the need to do social work outside of the church. We surely understand and confirm the need to be educated secularly and spiritually, since without knowledge we risk being aggressive and extreme. We believe we must have good relationship with government, and even cooperate in areas where the Holy Scripture describes."

These last two appendages seem very interesting as the first five grew out of early works by Mennonites and others, but these last two which really are a composite of a few post-Soviet feelings. For example, it would be impossible during the Soviet era to speak of the importance of education as it was denied to believers. The last point of government seems heavily orchestrated to ensure they are good citizens. The Russian church has always taken social work extremely seriously and the minute the churches developed they quickly launched missionaries. I would say, 90% of the Pentecostal pastors in Russia are from the Ukraine.

I find interesting the extreme emphasis on the apostolic message, order, and worship. It is interesting that premarital sex is tossed into the middle discussion but clearly has its place from the Council of Jerusalem in Acts 15. I can't help but wonder if these are more modern expressions, and that heavy use of the word apostle might grow out of Bishop Visley Evchick's visit to the Apostolic World Christian Fellowship. At any rate, the emphasis on apostolic is something we can all share and raises a point of discussion. Is this church apostolic? Are they holding to the Apostolic message? It is interesting that they want to be apostolic and yet apostolic as in Acts the second chapter where they continued in the "Apostle's doctrine". This group speaks emphatically about the Holy Ghost and the gifts of the spirit but say nothing about baptism in water and in Jesus name which is included in the passages. While they are not teaching the apostolic message on water baptism in Jesus name; they are also not denying that truth.

Voronaev would die in prison, and Smorodin would die in prison. So many would die as they stood for the faith. I remember in 1990 when I first met an apostolic pastor in Moscow, and with pride he spoke to me of the history of his church and he laid out on the table a series of pictures of pastors. He began the litany of this with, this was the first pastor and he died in prison, and this was the second pastor and he died in prison, and this was the third pastor, and so on. So, I can say this with great ease sitting here in my living room in air-conditioned comfort, but for them it was decades of real horrible suffering. Words cannot express, for so many of which multitudes of our brothers and sisters were tortured and died during the Soviet period.

I want to be sensitive in telling their history; they suffered so much. I am trying to simply make people here aware of many of our brothers and sisters that stood for God in terrible conditions.

Evangelist A. D Urshan in Russia

A.D.H. Resting
3/35

144

# Chapter five

## Nathaniel Andrew Urshan

## And

## The Collapses of the Soviet Union

An event was to occur July 1, 1951 that clearly represented what was happening in the old Soviet Union. It was the World's Trade Fair in Moscow, Russia and the United States had sent as its representative, the Vice President of the United States, Richard M. Nixon, and for the Soviet Union was Nikita Khrushchev. Each country had put up various items of their country's achievements, and in the United States Pavilion there was a new technology of color television by Ampex. An informal debate began to take place that was captured on film for everyone to see. Not only did it show clearly the contrast between communism and capitalism, but it captured the insecurity of the Soviets as well as their admission they were behind in economy.

There is a lot of bluster on the part of Khrushchev and an insistence that they are doing well, but also more than once he admits that the United States of America had a very high standard of living to which they had not achieved. In Soviet style he kept insisting that in seven years they will catch up with us and bypass us. Khrushchev in fact is going to learn a lot at this meeting, as well as his later touring the United States. Just watching the two on television makes clear the real differences in thinking between the Soviet Union and the United States. Among old Soviets, these views are still quite popular, not only the way they think, but the way they present it. At one-point Nixon says, "Don't be afraid of new ideas." One of the humorous times is when in American-style the Vice President puts him down, and he is not even aware, as the Vice President says, "this is what we have come to expect from the Soviet Union". His meaning was the arguments, the boasting, and the insecurity.

Khrushchev simply cannot believe that there is openness in America where we hear for ourselves what various leaders are saying and form our own opinions. He totally rejects the very idea that what he is saying will be heard by Americans. They even reach a point of agreement, and then starts off on another line about being a miner and working in the mines, and that he cannot agree with an American as the miners would be disappointed.

What is clear is that things are changing in the old Soviet Union. There is now a greater openness in the 60's, as one could not imagine Stalin debating an American leader, and there would be no place for discussion. It is also clear that they are way behind us economically and in the materialism that we have here in the United States- and they are hungry for it. The Iron Curtain is rusting away.

What this meant for the church was far less persecution and acceptance. From Khrushchev on, there will be greater tolerance, but there will be a great deal of blustering and from time to time persecution. Khrushchev will be on television holding the Bible up and say that he looked forward to the day when the only place you would see this book would be a museum. He would make speeches and talk about longing for the day that he would be able to introduce you to the last Christian in Russia. The irony of course, is that later his son will be a believer traveling across America speaking on college campuses to Christian youth. It will be during this time that many of the pastors that died in prison will be declared innocent even though they are dead. This is that rather stupid Soviet bureaucratic action that will make it easier on their descendants. Still, Christians will be rejected at work, and lose their jobs, demeaned as ignorant, and then they will be denied higher education. The fear of the Stalin years continued to hang on for decades. While there will be a certain amount of freedom they will remember the hard times and be afraid to be extremely open.

There's a great story about Brezhnev, he liked to collect cars and Pres. Nixon on behalf of the United States gave him a Lincoln. Brezhnev liked to drive fast, and he insisted on taking Nixon for a ride in his car. At one-point Nixon said that he was a very good driver because he did not feel he would've been able to have made that last curve. So, Brezhnev's mother came to visit, and he was showing her his collection of cars, to which she responded that it was all fine, but asked her son, "what if the Bolsheviks come back?"

Clearly things are beginning to change in the Soviet Union, but there were two things that were causing them to hang on to their past: Sputnik and putting a man in space, and a global spread of communism. Ronald Reagan was going to take both away and it was going to leave them with the question why we are sacrificing when we have no gain. Year after year, the Soviets would go to Red Square and see maps with various states showing red with the constant expansion of communism. Suddenly it is stopped, and Afghanistan is gone, and then Grenada is erased, and finally Nicaragua. It is clear that there is no expansion; things are going in the other direction. They had started off so strong in space, and now the United States was talking about a Star Wars type of defense shield. This caused the average Soviet to feel no need to stand in long bread lines to get the things they needed in life and sacrifice with no gain. The Soviet Union was collapsing and is about to be gone. It must be understood that the conflicts in Central America and the Contras were strategic to bringing down the Soviet Union.

The Stalin years were the worst time of persecution in the old Soviet Union. Persecution would be lighter but would continue even to this day. Khrushchev would continue to rant that he looked forward to the day that he could introduce you to the last Christian in Russia. People were forbidden to own Bibles and to worship freely. Restrictions were structured in such a way that you could have some worship. The State created the All Union Baptist Church and virtually every form of Evangelicalism and similar groups such as Mormons and Jehovah's Witnesses were crowded into this one church group. They all had to learn to worship together and live together. This meant that Pentecostals would be Elders in the Baptist Church. What they called worship was rather subdued and constantly watched by the secret police.

If someone spoke in tongues, that was proof of a mental condition and they could be sent off to a mental home. Police might break in the service from time to time and simply begin to beat believers. People were still arrested and sent to jail but for shorter sentences. If you were in school and you were a believer that meant your teacher had failed to do their job and they could be punished, and a principal had failed by having a teacher that had failed, and all these could be punished. This meant the teacher did everything she could to drive you out of school and indirectly you were denied education. You would never be selected for higher education because you were a believer. Unofficially some of these things are still reported in Russia today. Russia remains on the US State Department's list of Nations of Concern around Human Rights Violations in Human Rights as of my last visit to the White House in the first two years of the Obama administration.

Parenting was difficult in Soviet times for believers. They were denied good jobs, higher education, and with their strong belief in large families as part of holiness and to be a good Soviet; finances would be very difficult. It was hard to find a place to live as you could be rejected based on your faith. No Christian could live within 100 kilometers of Moscow. There were medals of honor given to mothers in the Old Soviet: Medal of Motherhood, Order of Hero Mother, and Order of Mother's Glorious. These would be denied to Christian mothers, or even worse, would be given to the mothers and then taken away. Far worse was the fact that their children could be taken away and put in an orphanage based on their faith.

The Soviet Union was collapsing and this harsh treatment of families of believers is going to give rise to an event in which the Holy Spirit would use Nathaniel Urshan to bring down the Soviet Union. Even though he was chosen of God and was the catalyst to precipitate a great event, it is likely that he died never hearing the full story. Even though he would be used to accomplish the opening of the door for the propagation of the gospel broadly across the Old Soviet Region when it was done; the story had not been fully told. He likely passed from this life not only not knowing what a success it was, but with lesser people ridiculing his actions. I was closely involved in the latter part of the story, and I did not realize what was happening until only in these last few years.

There is a very interesting thing that takes place in societies that are less totalitarian and that is people feel free to ridicule and question the greater the freedom, and greater the protesting. When you hear people protesting openly, showing their face and demanding that the government is too restrictive then you know they feel free to do this without anything seriously happening to them. During the Stalin era, no one protested, but from Khrushchev on we begin to see the churches taking a little bolder action. Pentecostals asking for their own worship service and their own praying houses (as they call their church building). In the early 1960s, Bible schools were established in the western part of the Ukraine. Pentecostals and Jews and others began requests to migrate from Russia.

In 1962, two of these families, Vashchenco and Chemykhalov, a group of about 30 altogether from the village of Chernogorsk;, Siberia, Russia requested to be freed of their Soviet citizenship and be allowed to leave the Soviet Union. The exacerbation of this conflict centered on a child being taken from the home and put in an orphanage. The families, in desperation, had decided to homeschool their children. When the family refused to surrender even one child to the state one of the officials ripped the baby from the mother's arm tossed it over the balcony killing the baby, and this made them even more determined to leave Russia. On June 27, 1978 seven members of this family fled into the United States Embassy in Moscow, Russia and asked for asylum. There is usually a ring of Russian police patrolling near the US Embassy, and unfortunately the embassy uses foreign nationals in American uniforms as a layer outside of the embassy. When these original eight members of the family approached the embassy, the police turned them away and denied them entrance, but in desperation they pushed their way through and were able to get on US soil. Having gained entrance, they would remain in the US Embassy for four years hoping each day to be able to leave Russia. As they pushed through to get into the embassy one of the children, a boy was grabbed and beat. Later, when embassy officials asked about the boy in typical Soviet fashion they were told there was no boy.

The story of these families is the product of the times. Peter Vashchenco was an outspoken advocate for freedom. This shows the changing of the time, because no one would let such boldness go unchallenged during the Stalin years. Peter said he never doubted they would get out of Russia; the only question was when this would happen. They had gone repeatedly to the US Embassy seeking a visa but not understanding the procedure that you had to have a family member send you a letter of invitation; they were constantly denied. Peter did this often enough that a friendly Marine taught him Basic English, so he was able to communicate. Forced to leave their village, they went nearly 2000 miles starting on a train and later denied the opportunity to travel on the train. They once walked 900 km (about 600 miles) to the US Embassy seeking relief. Family members were arrested and sent to gulags. They were beaten, and they were denied the opportunity to work, but now they had fled into the US Embassy.

This was not an easy choice as there were several family members with the Vashencos, and 11 family members with the Chemykhalovs (about 30 altogether). This meant the majority of these two families had been left behind, and they missed their children and feared for their safety. The only hope at this point was to maintain for the moment a high enough visibility that likely the government would do nothing until eyes were taken from them. Life was not easy for these dissidents/believers that were living in the basement of the United States Embassy. You can imagine how unhappy it was to have these individuals crowded in a room twelve feet by twenty feet and two beds and the inconvenience it brought about. It inconvenienced everyone around so that people were not always polite. There would be odors. Staff would constantly be complaining. With two beds they would have to take turns sleeping. In general, it was very inconvenient.

Nevertheless, they held on and stayed demanding freedom. There was a prayer group at the embassy and this provided them with some people that were very sympathetic to their plight. Over a period of time they were able to talk embassy staff into paying them for small jobs that they did, such as, wash cars, mend clothes, and other small task (this was personal money not provided by our government).

People in America hearing of this defection sparked interest among men such as Kent Hill and others. Nothing short of Providence itself could explain how rapidly all of this began to hit the news and bring about massive protest from the American people. Kent Hill was a key figure in all that was happening. He was a Fulbright scholar, young and energetic, and with great contacts. He would later hold key positions at Wheaton College, and later would significantly do great work in the world through the USAID. He wrote articles about it in publications such as Christianity Today, attracting attention to all that was happening very carefully. Through his efforts at Wheaton College, today there is a massive amount of records of everything that took place. This man was a driving force for good for these people.

Major US politicians, such as Sen. Jepsen and so many other senators began to pay attention to the point that by

November 1981, the Subcommittee on Immigration and Refugee Policy of the Committee of the Judiciary of the United States Senate held hearings and completely reviewed this matter with the extremely unprecedented measure of granting the Soviets permanent resident status having never been to the United States itself and was just one step away from granting them full citizenship. It is interesting that in the Senate report these Pentecostals were described as good people, and "almost saintly." They were in fact God's Saints.

Another man, hearing of their story and moved with compassion was Norman Rutzen, the United Pentecostal District Superintendent for the state of Idaho. He began to relate to everyone around him of what was going on in the Soviet Union. He was a driving force that kept saying to the general board of the UPC, "these are Pentecostals, these are our brothers and sisters, and we need to do what we can to help them." He pushed the General Board of the United Pentecostal Church on this issue and had a great ally in the General Superintendent Urshan. GS N. A. Urshan was called by his close friend Sen. Richard Lugar who urged him to go to Moscow and negotiate the release of these Pentecostals.

This is very important in trying to understand the White House involvement later. Remember, Sen. Lugar was a key figure on the Foreign Relations Committee and was chairman from time to time.

It was decided to send a delegation to meet with the Siberian Seven and push for their release. The group that went was the General Superintendent, the Foreign Missions Director Harry Scism, and the Foreign Missionary Secretary Robert McFarland. Norman Rutzen was invited to go along at his own expense. This made a representation of four men with three being the officials. There were no direct working relations between these churchmen and the State Department; however, the door to Russia was not officially open at this time. Men such as Billy Graham had made a trip; it even reached in the Baptist Church there.

This was all new and very exciting with the old Soviet Union being so closed and afraid of Americans. They knew they would be watched and listened to and that possibly their rooms would be bugged. Brother McFarland's wife purchased a few of the children's toy slates which you can write and then lift the sheet and it erases it, so they could communicate with each other without anyone hearing. Not that many traveled to Russia in those days and visas were extremely limited. Sister McFarland says that her bother and the others were briefed by the state department before they left and warned to be careful. They had been instructed that they must be very careful and understand that they were under observation at all times. Harry Scism told me that he had been told maids would go through their luggage in the hotel room, so he arranged his clothes in a very specific manner and when he returned to the room he found them different. They were observed in everything they did.

In their hotel room, Urshan and Rutzen while visiting went to move a coffee table, and they noticed it was unusually heavy. They looked under it and saw a large mechanical device for recording or broadcasting. Later they found a bug in the lamp. Likely, these were the ones that the KGB wanted found.

Later, on their return to the US, they would be debriefed by the State Department as this was one of the few very direct contacts between Americans and Soviet officials. This was truly historic.

Under the leading of the Holy Ghost, General Superintendent Nathaniel A. Urshan of the United Pentecostal Church, went to Russia to speak to these seven and visit with Soviet officials. On the plane in March of 1982, Harry Scism turned to the General Superintendent and asked who exactly we are going to meet with in the Russian government, and Brother Urshan replied, "The Holy Ghost is going to have to lead us to show us who to meet." This visit by Reverend Urshan and the other ministers would mark the first visit of American Apostolic ministers Since the start of the Soviet Union. However, there was no direct contact between these Apostolic leaders from America and leaders of Jesus name brothers on this trip other than the Siberian Seven.

In those days when one arrived in Moscow the things an American would notice first was the "dark oppressiveness." Dark oppressiveness was the very words used by Norman Rutzen to describe the general condition of Moscow. Young people and visitors today will find it amazing. Today, Moscow is bright, colorful, full of life, and has brilliant shops of all sorts to enjoy. At that time when you flew into

Moscow there were no advertisements and a few, if any, shops. The light bulbs were dim and gave so little light that it seemed it never reached you. It was very dim compared to what Americans were used to having.

Under communism, that country was not service oriented. The selections were limited, and you were seldom greeted with a smile. The state department had already warned these men that when the passport control person checked their papers they would look back and forth at them several times. All of this was an uncomfortable backdrop as an experience for these church leaders.

They were assigned an official Soviet translator that stayed with them at all times, they were watched and monitored, and meetings were set with officials. They were able to meet with the appropriate Soviet officials and asked that these Siberians would be free to exile from the USSR. It is reported by Brother Urshan that they met with a Soviet official who spent a great deal of time yelling. He was able to meet with this group at the US Embassy.

These four men in Moscow seemed handpicked by God with backgrounds that made them very unique to this trip. N.A. Urshan, the son of Andrew David Urshan, having such a rich background from his father ministering in Russia and the imperial days of that country with great revivals, and it had given him such a loving heart for the people there. Robert McFarland that had ministered for so many years in the Middle East and understood the mentality of autocratic governments. Harry Scism that had been raised on a Mission Field in India and had a global vision of the need of men for salvation. Finally, Norman Rutzen, a man that God had given a special burden for those in Russia and a great desire to fellowship with the underground church.

These four men were in Moscow and were being guided around the city and taken to see the usual sites. Passing through the entrance, they passed by the figure of General Zhukov that had led the Red Army in World War 2. At the entrance, there is a spot that marks the beginning of all mile posts in Russia. They would go into Red Square viewing the Walls of the Kremlin, with the Onion Domed St. Basil across the open plaza, and the GUM (Glavnyj Universalnyj Magazin –Main Department Store.) While touring GUM, they were in the department looking at fur hats when they heard a person speaking English. They engaged in a conversation and discovered he worked for the United States embassy. This man explained to them where the embassy was located, how to enter, and how to set a meeting. Harry Scism told me that it was at this moment he realized there was no plan, and that they would really have to trust God.

They went to the United States embassy and were greeted, as American citizens, as being on United States soil. This embassy in its construction had been so bugged that it was not safe to speak openly in this building. They were given the treat and honor of being taken into the bubble. This was a glass room so that you can look at the walls and see there were no listening devices. It was an area a conversation can be held without the Soviets knowing what was being said. Here, the second time, they were warned that they would be watched and monitored and that someone was always listening. They were told that they could be a danger to those around them after they left.

The State Department of the United States of America, through its employees at the embassy, would render assistance to these men by giving them the opportunity to visit with the Siberians in their basement and walking them through and providing the various forms that would be needed to request visas for these Pentecostals. There would come a moment when various groups were wanting to be the sponsor for the release and at the embassy this group would formally be asked who they wanted the sponsor to be, and they would say," Urshan."

In the embassy, in the small quarters set aside for the Siberian Seven these four men with the Russians would celebrate in a hallelujah, Jesus name, Pentecostal, worship service. Norman Rutzen on the guitar and perhaps Robert McFarland, the song leader and also playing a guitar-they would all worship God together. They would sing old hymns of the church and this was for two reasons as they needed some songs with which both were acquainted. One can sing in Russian and the other in English, and they all enjoyed the old hymns of the church, such as "At the Cross". Brother Urshan would preach as though he was preaching at general conference. Brother Harry reported that there was such a sweet presence of God. Much like any small home mission service except the prominence of the leaders and the setting being not a store front, but the Embassy of the United States of America. Just consider what God had done.

They visited with the metropolitan of Moscow seeking the assistance of the Russian Orthodox Church in releasing these people. They found a real coldness, and it was an apparent apparatus of the Soviet government.

They were received at the All Union Baptist Church where the General Superintendent was invited to speak. There was not the warmth that we would envision in our churches here for two reasons: the culture being far more formal, and the presence of the KGB with them. The translator, was of course, an agent of the government. At the time they visited there was always the fear of someone reporting some little transgression. Churches and church leaders had to be very cautious. It was quite a brave, new, and a brotherly attitude for this Baptist church to invite an American Pentecostal leader to speak from its pulpit. There was an openness taking place that had not been there in the past.

Norman Rutzen's great desire was to visit and worship in an underground, unregistered, and uncontrolled church. As such were illegal this had to be done in secret, but how could they do this with a minder following them around. They had met believers and had been told that they would be happy for them to go to church with them, but it had to be done clandestinely. Arrangements were made for the others to keep the minder busy as they would go into a store and begin to move around separately with one or another talking to the translator and calling them over. They moved out in a wider and wider circle within the store and eventually Rutzen slipped off to the side and out the door. Here he would connect with a believer that would take him down through the subway system and across town to a meeting where they can go and have a church service together.

Later, the four were taken to the various Soviet government buildings where they met with the proper officials. These were lower level officials when compared to the Foreign Ministry and they no doubt had no knowledge what was going on in the background. These men gave Urshan and his team no hope, in fact, the key person for the Soviets is reported to have turned red and screamed. He told them that the Soviet Union would never let these people go. Nevertheless, our heroes submitted the proper forms to the best of their ability, and this would eventually produce the desired result. This mission to Moscow can best be described as incredibly successful, would produce the release of the Siberian Seven, and eventually open the door for the gospel across Russia.

The doctrinal position of these seven would be later questioned, but you must remember them as being through the persecution of the Soviet Union. Remember, all faith groups had been pushed together and all of them struggled to hold onto their history, pastors had been put in jail, and they had been denied Bibles. They did not have the history that we have here, nor the conveniences of being able to draw hardlines. Even today, if you asked someone in any Pentecostal group in Russia," Do you believe in baptism in Jesus name?" They will automatically say they do, "Da, da." They will say it is Bible. They will say it is the Bible way.

This does not necessarily mean they were baptized in Jesus name, nor does it mean they weren't. They are not saying that they do not baptize also in the name of the Father, Son, and Holy Ghost. Remember, A. D. Urshan was a Pentecostal preacher before he got the revelation of Jesus name, and in that he is regarded as a pioneer of both the Pentecostal message and the Jesus name message. If you ask them, Trinitarian or oneness, do you know the name Urshan likely they would say, "Yes, yes that's us. We are Urshanites." They would know the name and they would've identified with Urshan very closely. This is going to cause those in the United States later to find fault with what took place and to criticize the action.

I am told by Nathaniel Paul Urshan that he spoke to these individuals about their doctrinal position, and that they were clearly of the Christian Evangelical Church of the Spirit of the Apostles. He further related that some were more religiously serious than others of the overall group, and that for some it was more about individual freedom, economics, and their own agenda, but at the core there were those simply wanting to worship God freely. Again, to focus too much on this is to miss the really great work that God did in collapsing the Evil Empire.

In the Embassy of the United States in Moscow, Russia, a worship service took place. With Rev. Rutzen playing the guitar and all joining in song, these four Americans and the Siberian seven began to worship God in Holy Ghost worship. There was a bond formed between Nathan Urshan and the Siberian Seven, and this was very likely because of the work that A.D. Urshan had done. A working relationship was established, and along with all the other voices the United Pentecostal Church cried out for their deliverance.

## God Using the President

All this had started under a very inept presidency of Jimmy Carter. He is no doubt a good man with well intentions, but terrible policies. They used to have the joke in his day that if he was elected president of Saudi Arabia there would be a shortage of sand. There were so many problems with high gas prices, a poor economy, and hostages being held in Iran. The Siberian Seven were simply one more problem for him to get around to someday. They were low on the White House priorities, considering hostages in the US Embassy in Iran. Despite all the protesting, the Siberian Seven were left to languish in the basement of the US Embassy for years. Ronald Reagan became President of the United States of America on January 20, 1981. This would immediately begin to solve several problems including the release of hostages in Iran that occurred the very second, he was sworn in as president of the United States.

I was standing on the Capitol lawn that day as the President was sworn into office. People were listening on radios at the same time and it was announced that the hostages were in the air and there went up a shout. This was a new day with the President that seemed to understand the world situation.

The President would go to the National Association of Evangelicals in Orlando in March of 1983, and he would describe the moral condition in our nation and the need for revival. He would define communism as the "Evil Empire." An extremely "Better Dead than Red" speech, he made it clear that faith in God was more important than simply being able to live if it were without faith. This was his early childhood religious training for which he was completely sincere. This was the first time that communism had been defined in public policy or by a major politician in Biblical and moral terms rather than simply differences in economic systems.

Very early in his campaign as still governor of California, men such as Herb Ellingwood advise the president that if he could get the Pentecostal vote he could likely win the presidency. Herb Ellingwood, Pat Boone, Harold Bredesen, and others of a Pentecostal or charismatic bent met with the then governor in Pasadena. Governor Reagan found these Pentecostals a natural ally, and he was very serious about Bible prophecy and the end time message. He related to these ministers how he had visited with Billy Graham recently, and that they had discussed the signs of that time. They began to discuss some of what the two of them had talked about, and one of the group interjected and said you have missed the greatest sign of them all and then told him, "In the last days, Sayeth the Lord, I will pour out my spirit on all flesh."

These persons laid hands on the governor and prayed for him, and Herb described how you could feel the presence of the Holy Ghost enter the room. Those praying noticed under the power of Jesus, his hand trembled and jerked.

The prayer concluded with the promise that God would put Reagan in 1600 Pennsylvania Avenue.

The strategy had been laid out that would later take him through Dallas, Texas with men such as Ed McAteer, James Robinson and the National Affairs Briefing that would propel him into office. The president had made promises and he felt close to his evangelical roots. The first thing he began to work on was a Constitutional Amendment for Prayer in School, He would speak more than once to the National Religious Broadcasters and the National Association of Evangelicals.

Secretary of State, George Shultz addressing a briefing

President Reagan together with his Secretary of State, George Shultz, decided they were going to collapse this evil empire. One weekend (February 12, 1983) it snowed in Washington DC and the president was unable to leave and go to Camp David and decided to stay home. George Shultz was just returning from China, and the two decided to get together for dinner. This was a special treat for the Secretary of State and his wife to dine privately with Pres. and Mrs. Reagan. Unfortunately, because of the informal nature of the dinner there are no pictures. At that dinner they began discussing the USSR and what their plans were going to be for the SALT talks. Schultz had established a weekly luncheon on Wednesdays with the ambassador of the USSR. He was relaying to Reagan his thoughts from their luncheon meetings, and he felt what was needed was to find some point, not too large, that they then push another, and another until eventually the whole system collapsed. As they discussed the matter, it came into their mind (I believe by the guidance of the Holy Ghost) to start with the Pentecostals. As they talked the Secretary of State realized President Reagan had never met a high Soviet official, and he asked if he would like for him to bring the ambassador over for a visit. Present Reagan was eager for this meeting, even though his staff was pushing against it. The meeting was arranged for the next Wednesday after lunch.

President Reagan in his presidential diary (Book of the President) would note that it had been squeezed in by saying he almost had forgotten the meeting (I suppose this is because it was not on the calendar.) The word I enjoyed in his diary was "sneaked". The President said that Schultz had "sneaked in" the Russian ambassador.

It was supposed to be a brief meeting (February 16, 1983) that turned into a two-hour session. Reagan outlined what a total and absolute disgrace it was for his nation to hold people that wanted to leave in such bondage. The President stated the suffering of these Pentecostals and that they should be free to leave. The ambassador explained (in his ride back with Shultz) something might be worked out, if the President would not "Crow" about his victory. Now here is a very important lesson in diplomacy that applies whether you're working with other governments or other church groups. You might be able to accomplish a great deal if you don't run around making the other person look small, or feel it was an "I got you" victory. It was here at this White House table that it was finally agreed that if they went home they would suffer no persecution but would be granted visas and allowed to leave Russia, but not to the United States. The timeline is very tight and no doubt this arrangement had been made prior to the Evil Empire speech, about the time they had gone home, and a couple of months before they would be granted visas. It would have been very politically popular for Reagan to have announced this at the National Association of Evangelicals. It is a big lesson that getting the job done is more important than crowing about it. Isn't that marvelous that was the ambassador's word − − crowing. I read in the presidential diary of some victory the president had gained and the word − − crowing − − was used a lot. Interesting, -crowing. Remember it was in March that President Reagan spoke to the National Religious Broadcasters and he said nothing about his victory.

After almost 5 years of living in the basement of the embassy on April 12, 1983, it was explained to them that they needed to go home; that nothing would happen to them, and that they would get visas. It was hard for them to accept this, and they really questioned it, but felt they had no choice and they departed. It was a joyous reunion with the whole family in their home village, and life settled back into the norm. The USSR announced the last week in June that these families were being permitted to leave the Soviet Union for an undesignated country. Even with visas there were still several technical problems that would have to be overcome in their traveling that other nations would help with but not advertise. Most of their travel expenses were paid by various groups that have been working on their behalf with some money coming from Ray Barnett in Seattle, and much of it coming from the United Pentecostal Church, -but others were involved. When they were asked directly who you want to be your representative, they made it clear that they chose Nathan Urshan and the United Pentecostal Church. Likely, this is because they had bonded, and here were names they were familiar with: Urshan and Pentecostal.

Acting foolish to the bitter end, Soviet border guards permitted them to take only one suitcase each. The little girl tried to hide her precious doll amongst her underwear, but the guards dug it out and searched it thoroughly and finally returned it, but they confiscated a guitar that the embassy staffers had given one of them. They left much behind to be distributed among family members, but their most precious possessions had been their Bibles and religious books which they intentionally gave to church members because there were such shortages of these in the USSR.

Urshan preaching at the Baptist church in Moscow

Red Square in Moscow

Urshan entering the American Embassy.

N. A. Urshan, Norman Rutzen and Robert McFarland working on the papers.

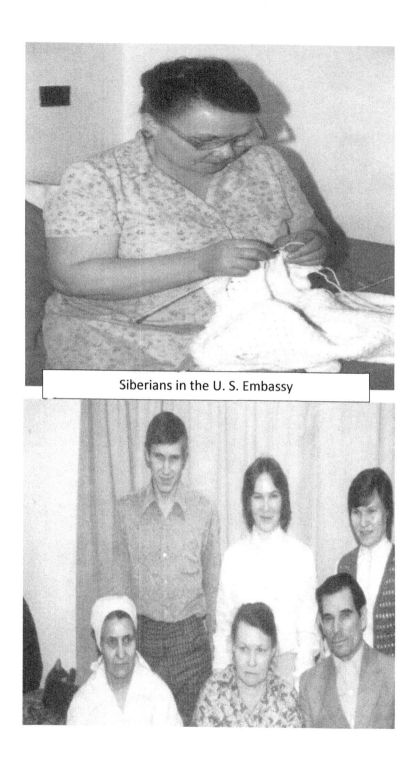

Siberians in the U. S. Embassy

Singing in the Embassy with the Siberian Seven, Brother Rutzen, Brother McFarland, Brother Scism and Brother Urshan.

N. A. Urshan, Norman Rutzen and Robert McFarland meeting with the Orthodox Church leaders.

While writing this section of the book I checked with Norman Rutzen, and Harry Scism which were both on the trip and present at all these meetings. Both were very cooperative and gave me all kinds of information. Norman Rutzen had written an article of everything that he could remember so that his grandchildren would be able to read it. He sent this to me and because it is a firsthand testimony I am including it without editing it, so you are given his firsthand witness, and it is as follows:

# SIBERIAN SEVEN & MY TRIP TO RUSSIA

## Norman Rutzen

When I sat down on that Sunday afternoon, I picked up the paper and the Parade front page story caught my eye. Seven Pentecostals from Siberia had rushed through the American Embassy gates and managed to get past the Russian Guards at the gate and reached the safety of the embassy and were directed to the waiting room. They requested to be allowed to go to the United States, so they could practice their religion freely. They had suffered much persecution and harassment in Siberia. The embassy informed them they could not send them to the US without proper processing. This would be a long process and would require processing through the Russian agency. They knew this was impossible and refused to leave the embassy saying they knew they would suffer greatly if they returned to Siberia. John the oldest son was caught at the gate and hauled off by the KGB. He showed me later the marks of his torture as the result of their action of going to the American embassy.

After refusing to leave and staying in the waiting area for several days, the embassy would not force them to leave the embassy, but they would have to stay in two small rooms in the basement until their situation could be resolved. They gladly went to the basement where Maria Chmykhalov and her 14-year-old son Timothy would stay in one room and Peter and Augustina Vashchenko would stay in the other room. Lyuba Vashchenko's youngest daughter, slept on the top of the washer and dryer and

Lydia slept on the concrete floor in front of the washer and dryer. They were visited by a few American individuals who tried to help their situation. They had written letters to the president and political leaders pleading their cause, but nothing seemed to provide any kind of resolution. The embassy was quite frustrated by not being able to resolve the situation and the Siberians refusal to leave.

## DECIDING SOMETHING SHOULD BE DONE

Moved by the tragic story of these Pentecostals I was struck with the thought of why Pentecostals in America shouldn't rise up to intercede for their Pentecostal brothers and sisters in this difficult situation. To them it was not an optional thing. They knew to leave the embassy would mean extreme suffering, and they felt they were as close to America as possible there in the Embassy.

I was on the General Board of the United Pentecostal Church at the time and the annual board meeting was coming up soon. I decided to present this situation to the board for their action. My presentation was well received, and a decision was made to send an official delegation representing the Organization to Moscow and hopefully get an audience with the government officials that could bring a solution. Nathaniel Urshan, General Supt., McFarland, Foreign Mission secretary, and Harry Scism, International Mission Director, would represent the Headquarters organization. I was invited to go with the delegation at my own expense.

# PREPARATION FOR THE TRIP

Excited to be able to participate in this challenging mission began to do all the background research and contact potential to help in our strategy. In the process I was contacted by a lady in New York when she heard I was going to visit Moscow on behalf of the Siberians, she inquired if I would be interested in contacting a Pentecostal family in Moscow that were also trying to immigrate to America. They were under surveillance by the KGB because they had been quite bold in their pursuit of religious freedom and attempt to get to America. It would require a willingness to take some risks and most of all not do something to further complicate or hurt their efforts there. They were participating in the underground church, so care would have to be exercised to not risk exposure to the precarious situation there. They communicated through letters carried by couriers because they could not risk any kind of postal or telephone communication. I sent my first letter to this lady that arranged the courier to get it to Moscow. I was so excited when I received my first letter from this family by courier.

It had been a desire for some time to be able someday to visit an underground church. I earnestly hoped this trip would provide that opportunity even though it involved substantial risk. It would also only be possible by invitation of a member of the underground church. If we could visit this family while in Moscow it just might be possible to get the chance to attend an underground service.

179

The time had come for the trip and I had prepared with items I felt would be useful to have a record of our experiences. A miniature camera and recorder and items for the Siberians. Before the lady in New York would give me the contact information for the family in Moscow, she wanted to meet me and get a right feeling that I would be the right person to open this door to. I totally understood her concern and I also wanted to assure her of my dedication to this mission and could be trusted. I flew early to New York and took a taxi to the address she gave me. It was apparently a business location several stories up in a business district. After visiting with her for some time, she said I feel good about you making this visit. She gave me several instructions and then said this is the code name you will need to make the initial phone call in Moscow. Don't forget this codename or you will not be received when you call. When you call, instructions will be given you as to how to proceed from there. I wrote this code name on the bottom of my foot while on the plane to Moscow as I didn't want to forget it. We had prayer together and I thanked her for giving me this opportunity.

I took the taxi to the airport and met up with the others and we were off to probably the most exciting experience of my life.

## OUR ARRIVAL

We arrived in Moscow and proceeded to the Metrapol Hotel which is directly across the street from the Red Square. Rev. Urshan said I would room with him and Revs. McFarland and Scism would take the other room.

We were shown to our rooms and procedures explained. We were given a room key which was connected to a tennis sized ball. It was really too big to put in our pocket and we were to leave it at a check station manned an agent 24/7 by the elevator and stairway when we left the room. It was a system used to know at all times if you were in your room.

We soon learned that people control, and observation was a constant thing. After we unpacked our things we checked out our room. I noticed the coffee table was really heavy. When we tipped it up to see underneath we discovered recording equipment that was recording all the time. Anytime we were discussing any important matters we moved away from the coffee table and turned up the radio so as to garble our conversation. We also found a miniature microphone in the ceiling light fixture in the bedroom. When we left the room each morning we arranged things in our suitcase and closet in such a way that we could tell if they had been searched while we were gone. Every day we were there someone went through our belongings while we were gone. This was one of the things that became a very irritating thing day after day.

## FIRST DAY OF THE EMBASSY MISSION

The first day was spent getting cleared at the US Embassy to visit the Siberians which were living in the basement of the Embassy.

After clearance at the main desk area, we were told we would be given a briefing regarding our mission and related issues regarding the Siberian Seven and their status. This had become a sticky issue between the U.S. and Russia. U.S. officials and congressmen had made individual and department appeals and efforts to gain their immigration to the U.S.

An appointment was set up for state department officials and ambassador to guide and prepare us for the meetings we had sought with soviet officials. The highest office we had gained appointments with was the Council on Religious Affairs that answers directly to the Soviet president. This meeting was set up for us in the "clean room" in a third-floor area in another part of the embassy compound. This was the area where a big international issue had developed because rays of some kind were being beamed into this area from across the street. We were escorted into the building and went through the U.S. Marine check point. We had to leave cameras and personal items at the desk. We were cleared for the second floor and preceded up the stairway escorted by Marine security. The second floor also had a check point as well as the third. When cleared on the third floor, we were escorted by officials into the clean room which contained a Plexiglas type room inside the regular room. It was a totally clear plastic cube which was sitting on clear plastic blocks with no visible attachments. This made it impossible for any recording or surveillance equipment to be placed secretly in this room. It was an absolutely secure meeting room (and probably the only one in the embassy.) Its only furnishing was a glass table and plain chairs. It was here that the embassy officials informed us of the issues surrounding the Siberian Seven and the underground Pentecostal church. This briefing was helpful to us to know protocol and things to be conscious of. It also gave us the opportunity to gain their understanding and confidence in our sincere concern for these Pentecostals and those suffering persecutions under the communistic system.

They gave us assurance of their understanding and stated concerns about our safety and security. They gave us good advice on things we should avoid and be cautious about and gave us numbers to call them if we encountered any threatening situation.

## MEETING WITH THE COUNSEL ON RELIGIOUS AFFAIR

Our next meeting was with the Council on Religious Affairs in an area not far from the Kremlin. We went to the designated area and waited for the Council to arrive. When they came we shook hands and handed them our business cards, our name, address etc. and also our position or title, (We were previous told to have these cards made as they would be expected at any government meetings.) We were then led to a table which had chairs close to the wall. When we sat down we had to push back the chairs against the wall to be seated. Then they pushed the table up against us, which was probably a physiological ploy to make us feel trapped and somewhat intimidated. It was a disturbing arrangement and if we would have allowed it, it certainly could have been intimidating. We all presented some aspect of what our mission was and a request for consideration of these Pentecostal believers. They informed us that these Pentecostals were trying to "twist or ring the nose" of the Soviet government, and it would not accomplish anything. I made a statement that there was a dark cloud of public opinion over the Soviet Union of people around the world because of the treatment of these believers. At that, the head man slammed his fist on the table and shouted defiantly at me, "Let their God deliver them!!" Following our deliberations, they stood up and pulled the table away from us, so we could get up. I looked him in the eyes and said, "God may very well do that Sir!" which proved to be exactly what happened. We shook hands, but it was very apparent that our presence there was a definite problem for them. They gave us no assurance that any intervention would be forthcoming from them. The underground (or unregistered churches) were a large problem and irritation to them. They were concerned about the anti-government motives and actions of which they had no direct access to monitor. Infiltrators constantly tried to get into these underground groups to monitor and document any anti-government activity or statements and give opportunity to prosecute these Christians.

## OUR VISIT WITH THE RUSSIAN ORTHODOX PIMAN

We were hopeful that this opportunity to meet with the head of the Russian Orthodox church could give us an avenue of help as the Orthodox Church works closely with the government. We were hoping we could persuade them to intervene with the government on a religious basis. We were met by a very reserved man who showed us to the meeting room where we waited for the Piman to come.

This man was very reserved, and we immediately could see he was not open to us or our cause. Later we were to learn he was the KGB plant to observe and know all that went on inside the church. The visit with the Piman was polite and formal. After the brief visit we were given the opportunity to take pictures with the gentleman and the Piman. We left feeling our meeting was quite fruitless and provided little hope of any help from the Orthodox leadership.

## OUR VISIT TO THE 'REGISTERED BAPTIST 'CHURCH

Sunday, we had hoped to visit the Registered Baptist Church. This is the church that many Pentecostals attend who do not want to encounter the risk and rigors of attending the underground church. The government permits this church to function but places government plants on the Pastoral staff to monitor all that goes on. This was to assure there was no anti-government expressions or actions. A government agent or KGB man serves as a pastor, attends all meetings, sits on the platform. This is known by most all the congregation but is the price that is paid to attend church without fear of punishment or harassment by the government.

Bro. Urshan had been given an invitation to speak briefly. This is the same church that Billy Graham had spoken at. When we arrived, Bro Urshan was taken to the Pastors area and we found our seats in the balcony which gave us a better place to observe the whole area. The choir sang beautifully. When they prayed it was like a low roar. All heads were down, and many had shaking hands but no one raised their hands or looked up when they prayed. It felt

185

like there was a fine line holding these people back from breaking free in the spirit, but of course knew that would bring about bad consequences.   Bro. Urshan preached a brief encouraging message.

We were invited to a brief reception following the service with the pastors. One pastor was very interested and understanding regarding our mission. A little later, another pastor told us, "don't pay any attention to him, he is from Ukraine".   The pastor who drove us back to the hotel engaged in a very interesting conversation.  He also told us who the government agent Pastor was.  It was interesting to see how all these things were carried out within the church.

It was also apparent at this meeting with the pastors, that the Siberian's situation was well known with them but was not anything they were going to give us assistance with.  It was a big issue but not one they could engage with because of the total monitoring they were under.

## OUR VISITS WITH THE SIBERIANS

It was a very moving experience the first time we went to the basement and were introduced to the Vaschenko and Chmykhaov families.   There were six of them as John Vaschenko had been captured as they ran through the entrance gate. He was imprisoned, beaten and tortured before making him return to Siberia.   They had lived in this basement for two years. There were two rooms, one bathroom and a washer and dryer in a hallway.  Maria Chymkolov and Timothy her 16-year-old son slept in the one bedroom and Peter and Maria Vashchenko slept in the other room. Lyuba slept on the top of the wash machine and dryer and Lydia slept on the concrete floor. When we were introduced to them it seemed like an immediate sense of trust and friendship was experienced. Many political figures had visited them from the states. We were the first Pentecostal delegation to visit with them.

After getting a little acquainted with them that first day, we noticed a guitar and suggested we sing some songs that they could sing with us. Some of the hymns were familiar to them and they could sing along in Russian. Lyuba and Lydia could speak fairly good English as they had worked hard to learn English to be prepared if they were able to get to the United States. They would sing in Russian and we sang in English. Most of these songs were the old hymns from hymnals. This became a daily part of our visit which meant so much to them to have a time of worship together.

We spent many hours hearing their stories and experiences of living as Pentecostals in that hostile environment. They told of the secret meetings in the woods where they would gather to worship together. Maria told of the ice being cut in the lake, so they could baptize her. They longed for the opportunity to live in a country where they would be able to live out their lives in freedom. America was their focus.

They soon learned the attention they had from governments and officials especially in the U.S. Lydia and Lyuba wrote many letters and appeals to congressmen, senators, government officials, and religious leaders all across the U.S. Many visited the embassy as a result of these letters and news articles from the United States.

We were invited to attend the Sunday church service in the Embassy that is attended by many of the Embassy staff, including the Ambassador. This Sunday Embassy meeting was a mixture of traditional and some contemporary music and prayer. The Embassy personnel were always very helpful and kind to us.

One night we stayed quite late. Dressed as we were, it was easy to detect we were Americans. Standing in front of the Embassy we tried to hail a taxi. Several slowed down and then sped on past us. It was too far to walk to the Hotel especially at night. Eventually one stopped and picked us up. Upon arriving at the Metrapol hotel, the driver in his broken English wanted to get Levi jeans from us. We informed him we did not have any with us, but he continued to try to get us to give him some jeans.

The taxi cars were very small and for four of us to get in them was a challenge. One day at the Hotel we got in a taxi. Bro. Urshan always sat in the front seat. I was in the back behind him. When the taxi took off the front seat apparently was not attached well to the floor and Bro. Urshan fell backward and landed on my lap. We managed to get the seat and Bro. Urshan setting upright again and it gave us a good laugh at Bro. Urshan's expense.

We spent many wonderful hours in the Embassy basement with the Siberians. We worked hard at compiling and completing documents to assist in their immigration. We wrote letters of invitation and sponsorship to assure all things were ready should they receive permission to leave the Soviet Union.

Unknown to us at the time was the fact that President Reagan and Secretary of State, George Shultz was working on this fervently. We became aware at a later time that Pres. Reagan had insisted that the release of the Pentecostals in the Embassy be granted before the treaty was agreed between Russia and the United States. (See Articles)

## OUR FIRST VISIT WITH THE UNDERGROUND FAMILY.

Shortly after arriving in Moscow and getting settled in the Hotel room I went out of the Hotel to find a pay phone to call the underground family. I didn't trust the Hotel phones. I dialed the number and I heard a ladys' voice answer in Russian. I said "Hello--this is--(and I gave the code name) The lady almost screaming said "I must see you!! I must see you!!!" I had been told by the lady in New York that she spoke fairly good English, so it was easy to communicate. She said "we must not speak long on the phone. Listen close to my directions." She gave me the name of the street and block number. She then gave me instructions how to find their building and entrance. She said, look for building Number. You will then find an aluminum book stand. There is a green door just to the right of it. Go in this door and then go to the 6th floor. You will see a door at the top of the stairs to the right--that is our door. She set a time we could visit.  I was excited getting back to the hotel room to tell the others of the plan.

The time came, and we took a taxi to the building number on the designated street.  We got out of the taxi and began walking, looking for the aluminum news stand.  After a short walk we spotted what looked like the described book stand, and as described a green door on the right side of it. We opened the door, and nervously went in.  We saw the small crude elevator and decided to take it rather than the stairway six floors.  It became totally obvious that had we not had directions we could have never found the family. This was part of the people control, and isolation of the people being exerted at that time.

A scary but humorous thing happened on the elevator.  We could barely squeeze on the elevator with us four men. Bro. Urshan was standing in the front by the elevator door. He pushed the 6th floor button and the very outdated elevator started up.  It got part way up and then stopped. We were already anxious and nervous about being in this area and Bro. Urshan became very excited.  He tried to push buttons and excitedly said, "we've got to do something!! Get this thing moving!!!" I think we wanted to laugh but knew that would be the totally wrong thing seeing Bro. Urshan in panic mode.  We all felt like it could be a trap or something to harass us. After what seemed a long time (in reality a short time) the elevator started up again and we got off on the 6th floor.

We knocked on the described door and shortly it opened. The lady was so excited to see us and welcomed us in. She turned and immediately did something to the phone which hung on the wall. She explained that the phones could be tapped, and they had a way of disconnecting them, so nothing could be heard through the phone.

We had a very interesting visit largely around the life of a Pentecostal family in the Soviet Union. They had two lovely children and it was apparent that they wanted their children to be well taught on biblical truth. They showed us the books they had made to teach their children Bible stories as they had no access to them in Russia. They would cut pictures out of magazines, catalogues or any printed material they could find and made interesting picture books portraying Bible stories. They had spent much time creating these books and kept them hid when not using them because they feared the house searches conducted by the KGB. If these books would be found by the KGB it could bring serious consequences for them.

We spent a very inspiring and informative visit with them and time had passed so quickly. Realizing the late hour and knowing that we would likely not be able to flag down a cab, they insisted on walking with us at least part of the way back to the hotel. Her brother who had come to be at our meeting stayed with the children, and we started the walk back to the hotel. We had not walked more than half a block when a police van pulled up beside us and slammed on the brakes. Several uniformed men (we didn't know if KGB or not) jumped out and headed toward us.

The ambassador had told us that our visit was well known to the Soviets and that we would probably be observed closely. He told us that if we encountered any suspicious actions toward us that we should immediately call the embassy. There was no way we could do that where we were. I was terribly alarmed and thought they would probably take us into custody.

Lydia (the wife) said to us, "keep walking, keep walking. We have a right to be here. Keep walking." So, we did. After a short distance they turned from following us and returned to the van. After walking with us about half way back to the Hotel we told them we would be fine and could return home. They stayed with us a while longer and then when they knew we could find the hotel for sure they returned home.

About a week after our visit with them, the KGB came to their apartment and searched their home. They tore up some of the floor and walls that they suspected were hiding things. They did find the bible story books and confiscated them. This was very heart-breaking to both the parents and the children. They had been accustomed to much harassment as Christians but losing these bible story books was very disappointing. They would begin to make new ones as they were determined to see that their children would learn the bible message.

## A CLOSE ENCOUNTER

One morning the others were going to do a little gift shopping, but I decided I wanted to visit more with the underground family than to go shopping. I chose to walk as I now knew the way to their house. The closer I got I began to notice the KGB officers standing on each corner and sometimes in the middle of the block in little glass booths. I watched closely and realized they were using their radios clipped to their shoulder and communicating with I assume their officers. It was apparent they were watching for me and would use their radios. The closer I got to the family building the more intense the observation was. It was apparent it would not be wise for me to visit the family. Their observation of me was so apparent that I felt I should contact the embassy. I didn't have a kopec (coin) to use the phone so I went into a store to get change (kopecs) to call. When I came out, I observed a group of KGBs had gathered across the street about fifty yards down from me observing me and conversing among themselves. I had a strong sensation that they were about to take action on me. I felt I had no time to call and contemplated what action to take. Just then a bus pulled up to the curb where I was standing. It was loaded to capacity. When the doors opened I made a quick decision. I determined to get on that bus as they could not see me from the other side of the street. I somehow managed to force my way through the back door which was packed with people. I still don't know how I managed to get on as it was full of people to the doors.

I had no idea where the bus was going but observed how far it went before it turned and I concentrated hard to keep my location oriented in relation to the direction of the Metrapol Hotel, so I could make my way back. I rode the bus a few blocks and then got off and made my way back to the Metrapol, grateful and much relieved I averted a very serious situation. I should never have gone by myself as you have no witness or verification of your action if you should be taken into custody.

My communication with the underground Pentecostal family prior to our trip to Moscow had stirred my hope of attending an underground church meeting. Doing this would entail a number of miraculous things happening and that it also had tremendous risks.

First, I had to be invited and approved by the pastors before I could go. I asked the family on our first visit if it would be possible for them to get approval for me to go with them the following Sunday. They contacted the pastor asking for approval.  The pastors have prayer on Wednesday and if there are any request to visit they pray and God gives them the guidance on the approval. They rely heavily on the guidance of the Holy Spirit on these matters.  They have to protect the church from infiltrators who then tell the KGB and the pastor is arrested and sent to jail.

I was excited when I received word Thursday I was approved. I had purposely scheduled my return flight late Sunday night to accommodate the possible visit to the underground service. But then had some apprehension of staying Saturday night alone in Moscow because the rest of the men were flying out Saturday.

While they were packing Saturday for their return, I went for a walk around Red Square.  On the far side of the Square, I was approached by two men. They asked in English if I would exchange dollars at a very high rate. We had been warned by the embassy to not do this under any circumstance as we could be arrested for illegal exchange. We had not been approached one time to do this while we were together, but the time I was alone I was approached. I realized how precarious being alone was at that time. It made me think again if it would be wise to go by myself to the underground church. If arrested, there would be no witness, nor would anyone know about my whereabouts. Yet I did not want to miss this once in a lifetime experience.

When I got back to the Metropol Hotel, the others expressed their concern of me being alone and tried to convince me to leave with them. I decided to proceed with my plan to go with the family to the church meeting the next morning.

They left, and I immediately was somewhat alarmed when I realized I was alone. I had read the accounts of other pastors who had been alone in Moscow. During the night, KGB agents would enter their room with a naked woman. She would throw off her robe and go to the bed, making it look like she was in bed with the pastor. They would take pictures of the startled pastor with this naked woman. He would be hard pressed to explain this picture. They would threaten to send the pictures to his wife and church or organization. They would force him to sign a document that he would never return to Russia or require him to do other things to keep them from ruining his ministry. In some cases, they had actually sent the pictures and caused irreparable damage. There was little a person could do when they had pictures of that compromising situation. Alone, I decided I would make it impossible for anyone to get in the room. I took the furniture and placed it against the door and across the room to the far wall. They could not break through the door without demolishing the door. I didn't do anything with the recording equipment concealed under the coffee table or the device in the ceiling light fixture as this could possibly trigger action on part of the security. I packed everything ready to leave. All I would need to do was grab luggage and leave for the airport. I decided to get some sleep because tomorrow would be an exhausting day. But sleeping was impossible. Torn between my hopes and dreams of observing the underground church and the risk it posed to my family and church and wrestled all night with the decision of whether to go or to give up the opportunity I had dreamed of. About 3:00 am, I came to the decision I wouldn't risk it. I had asked the underground family to help arrange it and they were so excited it was approved as they had never had a visitor from outside the Soviet Union. I knew they would be terribly disappointed. I had some things I wanted to give to the family and say good-bye to them. I would have to leave the Hotel by 5:00. My first challenge would be to get by the person who sat by the stairway and elevator to collect the room keys. It would be suspicious of me leaving that early with no luggage and would probably trigger surveillance. I prayed for God to go before and with me and guide me. I would have to trust the Lord to make a way to not get arrested or cause this family trouble. I wore an overcoat as it was quite cold. The room key was attached to a rubber ball about the size of a tennis ball, so you could not get it in your pants pocket. I paused for a brief prayer, locked the door behind me and proceeded to the elevator. I was surprised when I approached the monitor's table that he was asleep in a big chair beside the table. I took this as a sign the Lord was making the way for me. I quietly walked past him and went down the stairway as to not make any noise with the elevator.

In the lobby a uniformed watchman eyed me closely as I proceeded to the doors leading to the street. My next decision was to walk or take a taxi. I really dreaded thinking of walking in the dark that long way with the other encounters I had trying to visit the family earlier that week. But getting a taxi at that hour would be likely impossible. Again, I felt it the Lord making a way when I spotted a taxi a short distance from the Hotel. I had him stop a block beyond the family's apartment building, paid the fare and started the walk back to the entrance after seeing that the taxi driver had left and was not observing me.

When I knocked on the door of their apartment they were so excited to see me and welcomed me in and did whatever they do to the phone to secure being monitored. I immediately explained to them my concerns and would not be going with them. She urged me, "please, please, you must come! You must come!! We have never had anyone from outside visit us. It will mean so much to all the church. Please you must go! It will be all right, we will be with you!!

I could see the disappointment in their faces and immediately something seemed to tell me it was OK. I told them I will go, and I had to get back in time for my flight that night. They had me take off my glasses, gave me a Russian cap. They made me look as Russian as possible so as to not attract attention. I had my small camera and recorder which they told me not to take out of my pocket at any time. I was to let her do the talking and for me not to speak English where I could be heard. I was to stay close by her all the time. Her husband and brother would sometimes be ahead of us, sometimes behind. They had procedures for security that were important to follow.

They put on their coats, picked up the picnic basket with food and went out the door. They looked down the stairwell to see if anyone was on the stairs. The husband and brother went first, and I didn't see them again for some time.

We went through a maze of alleys, corridors, that totally confused me as to where I was. Where we were going was outside the city of Moscow where I was not permitted to be. It would be about two hours by bus, subway and walking.

When we got through the complicated walk portion, we arrived at a bus stop. They waited to board the bus until just before it pulled out. (this was to assure no one was following them.)

When we got off the bus we entered a subway station and proceeded to go to a waiting train. We were about to board when suddenly she turned and proceeded to the next car back. When we were seated she said "See that man in the car ahead of us? He is KGB. Now I can watch him! "

We rode for a substantial time and then got off and headed for the exit. When we came out of the subway station I was totally shocked. It looked like we had regressed 40 years. The buildings were old and dilapidated. The streets were dirty and full of potholes. It was such a sudden shock from the reasonably modern but drab Moscow.

We proceeded across the street and down to the corner where several buses were parked. I thought it was probably a bus salvage lot. To my amazement we boarded one of the buses and a little lady stood inside the door to take our fare. She was dressed in a coat that was almost rags, with patches of cloth and sewn tares. An old purse hung from her neck with leather shoe laces. It too was patched and tattered. It was such an amazing sudden change from Moscow. On the dilapidated bus ride, I observed a helicopter and aircraft factory which was an off-limits area to citizens.

At the end of the bus ride we walked for probably 20 to 30 minutes. This was a one-way two-hour trip to attend church. As we entered the village at several intersections she would say "See the man in the brown coat? He is a brother and is watching for us." This was repeated for about six blocks. These watchmen were watching to see if there was any KGB activity. If so they would signal from corner to corner and then the last one near the meeting place would run in and warn the people gathered and they would immediately get out their picnic baskets and appear to be having a diner gathering. This was apparently permitted, so as long as there was no church meeting going on nothing was done other than to intimidate or terrify them.

I had anticipated a secluded building isolated in some inconspicuous place. But we approached this substantial sized house and were met at the door. We entered a hallway off the first room, apparently a bedroom and it was filled with younger children. The next room was packed with teen-aged young people. Then the main room was a large living room literally packed with adults. They were sitting so tight I couldn't see what they were sitting on. When we squeezed our way toward the front where three seats were saved for us I could see we would be sitting on planks laid on buckets. The young brother apparently went into the youth room.

Seated across the front wall were seven brothers dressed in suit coats. These were the pastors. The first one was the main pastor followed by the succeeding six. If the pastor was arrested the succeeding pastor would move up and another pastor in training would be added. The last pastor would speak first for maybe 3-5 minutes, the next a little more and so on until the main pastor would give the main message. This way the succeeding pastors would get training and experience to be prepared in the event the pastor ahead of them would be arrested.

When they began to sing and worship it startled me because I had thought they would be quiet as possible. They sang so fervently and seemed happy to have this time together. Unlike the registered church where they mostly kept their face down, these believers lifted their face and sang from their heart. Their voices were beautiful.

After about an hour and a half the pastor said something to the gathered believers about me. My host translated to me that they were so glad to have me visit them and accepted me as a brother. He asked if I would speak to them briefly. I hadn't known what to expect as they had never had a visitor from the outside but tried to have something in mind should I be asked to speak.

I expressed my joy at being privileged to gather with them. I brought greetings and Christian love from their brothers and sisters in America. They seemed moved and blessed with my thoughts to them. I felt so humbled to gather with these believers who paid such a great price to serve the Lord.

My host explained that we would have to leave the service early as I had to return to Moscow to catch my flight home. (the service would last three to four hours). Before we had to leave the pastor said something again regarding me. My host explained that they accepted me as a brother and all the pastors wanted to greet me with the holy kiss. This she said is a high honor and asked if I understood. I said I did. She directed me to greet each brother.

I squeezed my way over to the first pastor. (I had been seated about 4-5 feet from the lead pastor.) He gave me a big hug and then kissed me on the mouth. It startled me, but I tried not to show my surprise. When I moved to the second one he did the same and kissed me on the mouth. All seven repeated the same kiss. Somewhat shocked I understood the honor of receiving the Holy Kiss.

I squeezed my way toward the door to leave and the pastor asked to speak with me before I left. We moved to the next room which was a small kitchen. He asked that I pray for him as he expected to be arrested shortly. They were sure there was an informer in their group but had not learned who it was yet. I prayed earnestly for him there in kitchen that God would strengthen and encourage him and give him grace. I learned that within two weeks he was arrested and sent to prison.

When we left my host said we did not have time to take the same way home. She would take me in a taxi and see that I got back to the hotel. She told me not to speak English where the taxi driver could hear us. It was too risky to be in that area where I was not to be. I would have liked to ask many questions after the experience at the service that day. My focus now had to be on getting back to the hotel, get my luggage and get to the airport without getting arrested for violation of my visa terms.

When we got within a couple of blocks from the Metropol Hotel she told the driver to let her off. She paid the fare and told him to take me to the Metropol. I waved good bye to this brave dedicated woman who along with her family paid such a heavy price to serve the Lord.

I will always be grateful for the kindness and courage she and her family showed me and made it possible to experience the underground church.

I continued to correspond with them through couriers. My efforts on their behalf was influential in them getting to immigrate to the United States a couple of years later.

## MY FINAL ORDEAL LEAVING RUSSIAI

I got to the airport and proceeded to the ticket counter. They checked my visa and the agent took it in an area out of sight. We had been warned about letting our visa being taken from us. I asked the agent to please give me my visa. "Nyet" he barked and ordered me to proceed through check in. I moved on through the boarding area, but no one would give me my visa. I looked for a phone but could find none. I asked at a concession booth to use their phone and all I got was "Nyet, no phone" I wanted to call the embassy which they had instructed us to do but now I could not get a phone to do so. I walked the perimeter of the area looking for a phone and realized I was trapped it seemed without a visa. With all I had been through the last 24 hours I was tired with no sleep the night before and emotionally drained with the full day of visiting the underground in risk of being jailed for violation of my visa for being out of the area permitted. I was exasperated and emotionally spent.

If I went through the exit door I was in an area in which I could not enter the airport again without my Passport. This was a holding area that your only way out was the airplane concourse. So, I thought the only thing to do was to proceed to try to board the plane without my visa and passport.

When my flight was called I proceeded to the gate area of my flight. I felt very anxious as to what would transpire. As I got to the plane, there stood a KGB agent who stared me in the eyes and gave me my passport and visa. It seemed like it was their final way of saying you're not wanted here and you are under our control.

Total control was what we had experienced in our 10 days stay there. It had an emotional suffocating effect. I was very exhausted and affected by the oppressive spirit that permeated the atmosphere at that time in Russia.

I will never forget the amazing sense of relief as the plane lifted off the ground. I actually felt like a heavy weight lifted as we left the runway. I was free from that dark oppressive atmosphere, but my heart ached for the multitude of Christian believers who were destined to live their lives out in that dark realm.

When the Siberians were finally permitted to immigrate, Jacob, John and Lyuba came to live with us in Caldwell. I was able to persuade the College of Idaho to give Lyuba a scholarship to pursue her education. To my surprise and because of the big publicity of them coming to our community the College of Idaho granted Lyuba a full 4-year scholarship with room and board. She went on to get her law degree and became a lawyer. She had never graduated from high school and was to a great extent self-educated at that point. The college waived her previous education record to grant her the opportunity to get her education. Jacob is married and works at an optical business making lenses. John is married and now owns a number of rental properties in California.

••••••••••••••••••••••••••••••••••••••••••••••••••••••

Conclusion of Brother Rutzen's stirring account of the trip to Russia.

The Vaschenkos were granted a visa first to the nation of Austria where on Monday evening, June 27, 1983, at about 6 PM they were met by General Superintendent Urshan. Almost immediately, they were taken to Israel on a three-month tourist visa, and they were shepherded about by Larry Reed who found them a safe house in which to stay and care for them during this three-month period. This meant the nation of Israel, seeing the persecution of these people, granted them help unofficially, and were working with the situation behind the scenes. This was all very clandestine activity, and partly it was not to crow or embarrass the Soviet Union.

Today, many might wonder why clandestine activity, and why Israel and Jordan might be involved in helping with the situation. You must remember the context of the time. No one was allowed to leave the Soviet Union. It was not as Pentecostals, but also Israelis, and other minorities that were restricted and under persecution. Israel would not want to openly engage against Soviet Union because it might make things worse on those that were Jewish back in Russia. If the Pentecostals were able to leave it would be opening the door where all minorities could petition. Two years later, I asked to be able to meet with the United States ambassador to Russia and pray for him. I was granted this audience via the State Department. As a humorous side note the contact was made from the Russian desk at the Department of State and when the staff in Russia asked why I was coming to pray, the response was "that's what he does." Before he came in a young lady on his staff met with me and I assume they thought I was coming to petition or someone to be able to leave the country. She said, "It is my understanding that any Pentecostal and Jewish person that has requested a leave has been given permission." I explained I had no idea but was simply there to give thanks to God for opening this door and give thanks for the embassy and ambassador in their work.

Those that worked on this, some of those names are not mentioned because of the nature of the societies in which they are ministering, but the leaders in these countries know who they are and what they have done; they should see them as not only heroes of Pentecostals, but of Israel and Jordan and all those that desire a more stable region. It is true their efforts- the work of Nathaniel Urshan and all the others that opened the door for a tremendous Jewish migration to the nation of Israel, and Pentecostals to the United States, Canada, England, and many other countries. This was not freedom for just one group but for many, and I would be called on from time to time to speak to the White House about the needs of Jewish people as well as our own. You can imagine what a joy it was to be in Israel after the years of oppression and the Soviet Union. This was the land of their Savior, of Moses, and so many things that they had read about in the Bible. There was the sunshine, ice cream was very popular with them, and they toured the sites. They were looking very seriously at Israel and beginning to think of it as their home, but this would only be a stopover to clear paperwork for them to be allowed not to come from Russia to the United States of America, but to come from Israel here. The Chmykhalov family was not given exit visas until later, and by this time the USSR had seemingly come to understand there was more than one route to the United States and it was futile to not permit them to go directly there. They left Russia on Monday, July 18, 1983, and arrived in St. Louis Missouri on Tuesday, July 19, 1983. There they were greeted by almost

400 persons, virtually all Pentecostal, and including officials of their church organization. They came to the United States where Nathaniel Urshan had organized huge fund-raising rallies for them, and many gave. The United Pentecostal Church was noble and following through with all its commitments to these people, locating them in homes in the St. Louis area, and the Northwest of the United States. These were just simple every day American citizens wanting to do something to help these individuals that had suffered under such persecution. People gave massively; wanting to help these individuals relocate. Later, the President of the United States would speak to the fact that such actions were an extreme contrast comparing the suffering of what people went through under communism with the generous help given under capitalism. This would be a Speech that Reagan would make concerning Central America but is applicable here as well.

President Reagan addressing a White House Briefing.

All this was just the start of something much bigger that would very shortly collapse the Soviet Union. This was the first domino, this was the beginning point, and God had used Nathan Urshan and the United Pentecostal Church to bring this about. It is sad that General Superintendent Urshan died not knowing fully what he had done. He understood that he had rescued the Siberian seven and began to open the door for contact with Pentecostals from this country in that country, but not the full significance of those events. The USSR constantly accused believers in that country of working with Americans who were trying to destroy their way of life. If "by way of life" one means, the gulags, the denial of religious freedom, the harsh treatment of believers, the hostility toward the good, and the general lack of freedom, then yes, we were involved in calling for a better way of life. Our President had declared the USSR the Evil Empire. Thomas Jefferson had said," I have sworn upon the altar of God, eternal hostility against every form of tyranny over the minds of men." The battle was for the minds of men, and their souls. Often, we try to sugarcoat this claim we are not involved in politics of any sort. The fact is when you say that Jesus died for all men you are declaring them equal and this is also a political statement. When you say you are saved by grace then you are denying the state church. When you say God is Lord of all in a country that says there is no God; you have taken a political position. This was the beginning of something big in religious terms, it was the start of revival. In political terms, it was the winds of freedom. This freeing of these people was a monumental event.

The Bible says, they that have turned the world upside down come here also. You see Satan comes to seek to kill and destroy, and when he has his way men live in poverty and distress and their world is upside down. When you come in with the gospel and begin to preach hope and set the world right side up for them you are turning it upside down. I suppose if we were honest; the preaching of the gospel is incredibly political. It goes to the very heart of policies and raises leaders up and sets others down. The good news is at the core about salvation, but it affects so many other areas. Women's rights are an outgrowth of the good news. Simple Scriptures such as "the men and the women together," and "if a woman prays or prophesies. . ...." Just simply by reading of Scripture you offer hope to individuals that can change a society. Literally, it is turning the world upside down for them. We want to say, no, no, no, we are only here to offer salvation, but the reality is we bring the word of God with us. Dictators be they English Kings, or Islamic despots are threatened by the Bible. You can say what you want, but if the Word of God is preached it will bring change, and it is a political aspect. This was in fact such a monumental event, as the release of the Siberian Seven, that many of Urshan's own group have tried to play it down or snipe at it. They would question his taking them around the nation raising money for this group to settle into the United States. They would question them going off to live with other groups and not become a part of the United Pentecostal Church. They would be looking at small things while on the international stage huge things were happening that they were completely missing. They were small minded people that questioned these people. If they had lived in the days of Esther they would've complained that she was married to the King, a heathen. If they lived in the days of Daniel they would've complained, they should've made a bolder stand. Small minded they would miss the glory of what God was doing through great men.

Father and son leaving the hospital, .A.D. Urshan and N.A. Urshan

Nathaniel Urshan was the son of Andrew David Urshan, the Pentecostal pioneer and global traveler. His life and development were that of a mix with his mother leaving the family at a very early age to his father being extremely successful. Sometimes raised in more rural areas such as Saint Paul, Minnesota and other times in urban areas such as New York City. Being treated almost a prince in the church, and as an immigrant in daily school life. Teachers questioning why he was not taking Jewish holidays off, and his having to explain he was not Jewish but Persian. His childhood life was a mix, and it created a certain bitterness that caused him to want to escape the church. Like his father, he had a troubled youth but hid it under the guise of being seemingly successful-a minor league ball player, in training to become a medical doctor, and his father praying for him constantly. Young Nathan, during medical school, contracted TB while standing close to a cadaver that was being opened and not realizing it was bloated. He was miraculously healed and gave his life to Jesus and became a preacher of the gospel.

Young Urshan in the hospital.

Handsome, charming, and well-educated he caught the eye of Jean Habig of Indianapolis Indiana. The Habig family of Indianapolis were well known for owning a grocery store that gave credit. It is said they kept many family's going during the depression. One of these was my mother's family, but as my brother Danny says, "They kept most of the Southside going." The Habigs helped found Calvary Tabernacle of Indianapolis. Calvary was an outgrowth of the baptism of G. T. Haywood on March 6, 1916 - a month and a few days earlier than Andrew David Urshan being baptized in Jesus name in Russia.

Here we should take a little time to reflect on G. T. Haywood and The Pentecostal Assemblies of the World. This is the seedbed in which so much of the apostolic revival will grow. G. T. Haywood was a Pentecostal pioneer that would have been very active in the development of The Assemblies of God. He had joined The Pentecostal Assemblies of the World in 1911. It would be incorrect to speak of this group as either Jesus name or Trinitarian as it predates the controversy. That it was simply one of those groups trying to promote the Pentecostal faith. Haywood, like Urshan and the others, was slow to respond to the new Jesus name message. In 1916, Glenn Cook was holding a revival and preached on the subject of Jesus name and through their conversations he caught a revelation of this truth. And in March, 500 persons that attended his church followed him in the waters of baptism with the name of Jesus called over them. The sheer magnitude of numbers made this one of the largest Pentecostal church groups of its time. Despite its size and numbers, the church had never purchased a building. Things were about to change, there seemed to be a restructuring of the PAW in 1917, and Haywood was given the title Field Coordinator. Because, the PAW had been registered and in existence for a few years, it had a history that was recognizable for military deferment and discounted travel on railroads. This meant, for the moment the PAW was the leading apostolic organization in the nation.

G. T. Haywood was well positioned to take this leadership. By 1919, he had bought a building which would house the church and become the headquarters of the PAW. His church, now named Christ Temple, would be the mother church of the apostolic movement. This seems to be a reorganization again in 1919 or 1920 of which G. B. Rowe, Stanley Hanby, and of great significance Andrew Urshan will be on the board of Bishops.

Two major events would occur in 1931, one being the death of G. T. Haywood, and the second being the merger of the PAW, and the Apostolic Assembly of the Jesus Christ and renaming the group the Pentecostal Assemblies of Jesus Christ (taking portions of the name of each group to make the new name.) Everything about The Apostolic Movement is reminiscent of the Radical Reformation, and is accordingly, antiestablishment. Often accused of being a cult, it is in fact just the opposite. Within the fabric that makes up people that believe in the Oneness, baptism in Jesus name, and the belief of the Holy Ghost speaking in tongues is a pantheon of so many organizations, and these are constantly, merging and splitting, and developing new ones so that one would need a scorecard to keep track of them all. Attempts have been made to bring everyone together in such fellowships as the Apostolic World Christian Fellowship and organizational leaders are constantly trying to bring everyone together. The one positive of all this is that clearly the leadership is not singular and absolute. G. T. Haywood, Andrew David Urshan, G. B. Rowe, and others were able to hold the early movement together purely based on spirituality of themselves and the revival.

In 1920, the Ku Klux Klan controlled Indiana politics, and it was in this backdrop that Haywood was able to build one of the largest churches in Indianapolis, and it was interracial. Early Pentecostals preached the Holy Ghost revival as having great sociological impact such as, equality for women including women preachers and pastors, and the eradicating of race barriers. Both at Azusa Street and Indianapolis there was great celebration in the fact that race did not matter. Sadly, much of this has been lost as we have grown in numbers in churches. The 1930s seems to be the time when divisions started to take place.

But for the 1920s, there was this great interaction between Andrew David Urshan and G. T. Haywood with both working tirelessly to develop and promote the message. This would put the Urshan family around Indianapolis from time to time over the years. Today in Indianapolis, the number of apostolic churches is large. Despite their racial division and the organizational differences, ministers and church members can generally move from church to church and organization with great ease and acceptance. Churches today are again embracing a greater interracial nature and the church; it seems to be for greater growth for the future.

All this background will produce an interaction between the Urshan family, Indianapolis, and the early apostolic movement. This interaction will produce Christ Temple, Calvary Tabernacle, and make Indianapolis one of the leading centers of the Jesus name revival.

To understand Nathaniel Urshan, you must understand Calvary Tabernacle and to understand Calvary Tabernacle you must understand the Habig family. Andrew and Hatti Gakstetter Habig were strong proponents of the Apostolic Faith in the early days of the revival. I heard him speak of praying until the sun came up at the church and leaving to go open the grocery store. In 1932, the church that would later be Calvary Tabernacle was opened on Prospect Street. It seems strange, even to the Apostolic's today, that in the early days Apostolic's would not name a church, but rather simply give their location. It should also be noted that the founding of the church is within one year of the death of G. T. Haywood and lost to history is any possible connection. It is an interesting fact, that founding families in this church were descendants of founding families and members at Christ Temple.

Within a few years, Calvary would buy an existing church building on Fletcher and Cedar and take the name Fletcher Pentecostal Church. Over the years the city would grow up around Calvary Tabernacle in the city that would become known as a crossroads of America, as a church located where Interstate 65 crosses Interstate 70 and makes the church at the crossroads of America. Symbolically, when one preaches at Calvary Tabernacle that one is preaching to the nation. The Habigs would sign the note to purchase the new building.

The first pastor, Oscar Hughes, served during the time of the depression and all the struggles of those days for three years. He would be followed by Oliver Fauss, having greater prominence as the General Superintendent of the United Pentecostal Church later in life. After almost two years of service he moved to Houston, Texas, where he founded an enormous church that is pastored by his son today.

In 1937, the church would select Raymond Hoekstra as the new pastor. He was only 21 years of age but extremely energetic and produced dynamic growth. Under his leadership the wooden church building was torn down and a concrete block building was erected that could seat two or 300 people. Chaplain Ray, as he was later known, would pastor there for 10 years and left behind as his greatest accomplishment-Jean Habig. He had encouraged her to sing publicly and given her the first chance to sing at Calvary and promoted her. She would have been 11 years old when the new church was started and, 16 when Hoekstra became the pastor, and 28 when Hoekstra resigned to make room for her husband as the new pastor.

I have heard her speak of listening to radio programs that she can catch late at night and hearing popular singers that helped form the style she would develop. She had an incredible style of singing that would set her apart. In 1938, Hoekstra invited her to accompany him to New York City where he would preach, and she would sing. There she would meet the internationally famous Andrew David Urshan, but even greater significance his son Nathaniel. These two-young people had the pedigrees that made them of great significance in the new apostolic revival and it could be said their marriage of two years later was made in heaven.

The two would evangelize with some assistant pastoring for the next six years, and in 1947 he was invited to become the assistant pastor of Calvary Tabernacle. In 1949 at the suggestion of Raymond Hoekstra and with a nearly unanimous vote he was selected the new pastor of Calvary Tabernacle.

Nathaniel Urshan was 29 years old when he began to blossom forth as he became the pastor. He will pastor Calvary for close to 30 years, and over that time the church will grow from a regular Sunday attendance about 200 to more than 1200. Its growth will not be just in numbers but in influence with the street next to the church becoming Calvary Way. Influence in the community will grow to the point that he will dine with significant persons such as Uthant of the United Nations, senators such as Richard Lugar, and meet and talk with Presidents of the United States such as George H. W. Bush. Pastor Mooney related to me an incident when he and pastor Urshan were walking down the halls of one of the congressional office buildings and a congressman hearing his voice came out and grabbed

Nathaniel giving him a hug and picking him up off the ground. It was just this kind of informal, positive relationship he had with great notables. In fact, he had so many occasions to witness to great men over the years and such tremendous testimonies, lesser men of questionable talent would challenge his testimonies by saying "Always a whale and never a fish."

Brother Urshan set a standard for the church and for the future that is marked as a premier institution. He was followed by James Larson, grandson of Andrew David Urshan, who pastored the church for 10 years. James Larson built a whole new edifice that will seat 3,500 people and built the congregation by adding hundreds of people.

Father and son, A. D. Urshan and N. A. Urshan.

N. A. Urshan and Jean Habig Urshan

The Wedding of N. A. Urshan and Jean Habig

Pastor Paul D. Moony, an incredible visionary like the previous two pastors, took the present-day church, Calvary Tabernacle, to new heights. He filled the present building, purchased land for a great expansion, established Indiana Bible College, built an incredibly modern building for Calvary Christian School, and purchased the land needed to bring these institutions together at one location.

Under the leadership of all three men the grade school has developed into the finest private, Christian school in the state. Pastor Mooney established a Bible School for training of ministers and church leaders. I have known closely all three great pastors of this church across my life and Brother Mooney is the finest of the finest. All three are exceptional. Brother Urshan, as well as the succeeding pastors, became incredibly influential in the community and used their influence for the good. Nathaniel Urshan served on charities and on the international board of the YMCA. He would often tell gatherings at the YMCA that he appreciated all they had done to help his father when he was a young man with a place to stay and help him assimilate into America. He would also lead the United Pentecostal Church in doing social good and humanitarian assistance.

In fact, N. A. (as many called him, but never to his face), was going to lead the international church for many years in both significant humanitarian help for people, such as, Prudencio Baldedano; as well as, having a great influence on national and international public policies. I was going to have the privilege of working very close with him in these matters and being a witness to them.

Nathaniel A. Urshan became my pastor in 1949 when I was four years old and would remain my pastor through my life until his death. I have always considered Calvary Tabernacle in Indianapolis, Indiana, as my home church where I was a graduate of Calvary Christian School. In my youth, we were known to call our pastor "Dark Eyes"; this was because of his dark piercing Persian eyes that seem to follow you wherever you went in the room and gave the impression he knew exactly what you were doing. Later in life, he and I would have a very close working relationship although our agendas were individual but compatible. We would share many wonderful experiences, such as sitting in box 1, on the platform at the Capitol when President of the United States, George H. W. Bush, was sworn into office, and we traveled the world and shared in many common concerns. His mind was always working for the good of his organization, the United Pentecostal Church, and his nation.

It is about this time that I enter the picture feeling led of God to go to Washington D.C. to represent the Apostolics in the area of public policy to the White House to the Congress. How I got there is one of those pilgrimages that God leads us through. I had witnessed to the student body President, David Warnick, when I was at the University of Idaho. I watched him receive the Holy Ghost speaking in tongues. Upon graduation he went to Edinburgh, Scotland, on a scholarship and while there became very excited about the conservative movement of Margaret Thatcher. He had been the president of the Republican Youth at the University of Idaho. When he returned to the United States he became the campaign manager for Newt Gingrich and I had gone to visit him in January 1991 not realizing it was Inaugural Day.

On a second visit with my brother Mark it was suggested we visit Bob Sweet, Special Assistant to the President, at the White House. We entered a conversation concerning our faith groups-what it meant to be an apostolic. Bob asked who was representing us in Washington D.C., and I told him really no one. I was recruited to begin to develop a plan to open the door to invite apostolic leaders to the White House, and to give us equal access that so many other groups enjoyed. This liaison work goes back to the very foundation of our Republic when George Washington received and entertained such church leaders as George Whitfield. The Constitution does not prohibit nor promote faith. It simply grants that whatever one church receives all must receive, and that all stand equal. Of course, a President, a Senator, or a Congressman may have a very specific religion, and openly practicing it, and announce it. Jimmy Carter claimed to be born again, was a Baptist, and taught Sunday school. Most Presidents had declared a specific religion.

I'm not going to spend much time giving detail in this book about my life in Washington D.C., as I will save that for the next book. It is about this time that, N. A. Urshan and I began to work actively together on several projects. When I went to Washington I was received with open arms and I did not know until much later, till even now, why I was so popular with people such as Faith Whittlesey. It was because I was Pentecostal, and this meant several things; such as, what was happening at the State Department and their plans for Russia, and that this was a major group that was influencing the political scene in elections.

I began to work closely with Carolyn Sundseth, and her bosses Morton Blackwell and Faith Whittlesey. I began to bring groups of church leaders to the White House. I started with the Assemblies of the Lord Jesus Christ. God worked an incredible miracle on this first briefing at the White House (a briefing is when they give you key speakers that explain the situation that is going on and what is being done and how our group can help.) At our first briefing was, Major Oliver North, speaking to the threat globally from the

Soviets, a spokesperson for Jeanne Kirkpatrick on the UN and international affairs and Robert Sweet, for domestic policy. It was here that I heard, Osama bin Laden's name for the first time. Col. Oliver North said he was the most dangerous man in the world, and this was a time when few had heard that name. We were hosted to a lunch in the Old Executive Office Building. While we were dining, Morton Blackwell came in to join us. He apologized stating that they were working on the prayer amendment and that many denominational leaders gathered to meet with the president. He then turned to Don Johnson, the General Chairman of the Assemblies of the Lord Jesus Christ, and asked if he could get him clearance, would he go over and meet with the president. This was the first official meeting of an apostolic leader with the President of the United States – – that is as the Chairman of the Assemblies Lord Jesus Christ, he was meeting as a representative of that group with President Reagan.

God has a strange way of working things, because we were having this briefing and because we were going to dine with Morton Blackwell, it turned into Don Johnson going over to meet not only with the president but with other church leaders such as, Jerry Falwell and Thomas Zimmerman. Because it was at the last minute he was seated at the far end of the table so that the picture of the event is not clear except to those that know him well and recognize his profile.

Don Johnson, Vice President Bush and Stanley Wachtstetter

Don Johnson leaving meeting with President Reagan and Christian leaders, meeting Stan Wachtstetter at the W. H. gates.

Also, arriving much later was a rather rattled, Jimmy Swaggert. By the time Swaggert arrived the rest of our group had positioned ourselves in front of the North gate of the White House and were by the security checkpoint where he would check in. I went over to shake his hand and I remember the guard asked for his ID and he gave them his American Express card and I told the guard you must know who this is. What this did was open the opportunity for me to introduce myself to him and give him my business card.

This then opened the door for Don Johnson, Sheldon Young, my son and myself to visit Jimmy Swaggert at his operation in Baton Rouge, and there at length we discussed his booklet **The Error of the Jesus Only Doctrine,** and I was able to present our view of the Bible to him.

Stanley Wachtstetter, Don Johnson, Jimmy Swaggart and Jon Wachtstetter.

That meeting with him and the president would springboard me into liaison work between the White House and all apostolic groups – – we termed this "the Apostolic Coalition." This was not lobbying in the traditional sense but was simply a representation of the worldwide revival of the Holy Ghost in Jesus name before civil leaders. This was an opportunity God gave me to be able to represent the name of Jesus broadly. It also placed me in a position where I was able to meet with and discuss our doctrine with almost every significant religious leader of the day. As this representative I would be called on by Carolyn Sundseth to share with my understanding of where the churches stood on various issues.

As an outgrowth of this meeting between President Reagan and General Chairman, Don Johnson of the Assemblies of the Lord Jesus Christ, the first issue of which I began to work was the Prayer Amendment. This was a real learning experience for me. With something like 85% of the American public wanting prayer in school it would have seemed an easy issue to promote. There are however, forces in Washington that have their own agenda and they play a mean game. First, it was passed in the House of Representatives, then it went to the Senate. Again, this should have been a very easy passage, but there were a few states so far to the left that they did not want this passed and thus you have a few senators ready to vote against. Only one-third is needed to block the passage of an amendment and thus the game was on, with virtually all those ready to be elected in two years voted for its passage knowing the American people would likely vote them out of office in their anger for voting against this amendment. Of the next third, there were a few more than voted against it and were likely planning on not running again, and finally the last third that would not be up for election for six years. There was a larger group that voted against this assuming the American public would forgive in six years.

President Reagan was extremely serious about these religious matters and among his greatest concern was the

American family, and prayer in school. He was right, and you can track the change in society from the moment the prayer was taken out of school. He knew his Bible as his mother was a preacher of the gospel and would go into jails and preached on the street. She would take in girls that were unmarried and pregnant and would work with them trying to get them through the trying time.

Liberals, such as Norman Lear would attack him, name calling him - -the Evangelists in Chief of the United States of America. The President was a firm believer in prayer and had an appreciation for the church people and their support of what he was trying to do.

The President of the United States had declared The Soviet Union to be an Evil Empire. This was now official state policy. It was clear that the Soviets were not limiting themselves to their region but were active as close as Cuba in Central America with listening stations in Cuba and another massive one being built in Nicaragua.

In every governmental system there are various views that are constantly pulling against one another or working together. This is true be it a school, a church, or a nation. In national politics there will be forces that will want to pull in one direction and others in another. In the USSR, Gorbachev had established *glasnost* and the *perestroika*. This was not an easy fight for him as the hardliners kept trying to push back towards a more Stalinist view. This created great tension and there was a constant undercurrent of a crew to displace him.

Since the time of Khrushchev, the USSR was constantly opening and becoming more tolerant on its citizenry, and it seemed to be fighting for its very existence as it was old, inefficient, and creating greater poverty every day. In this, the pressure had to be kept on, especially in Central America. The Soviets were losing the war in Afghanistan which had become their Vietnam. Central America was a place in which they were struggling for growth. It's a fact that growth was what the hardliners could argue to keep the old Soviet going more years. This was a brutal and repressive regime that killed scores of millions of Russians and was carrying that brutality out around the world. It was the "Evil Empire" and needed to be stopped.

By this time, Faith Ryan Whittlesey, had asked me to serve on a Working Group on Central America at the White House where we met every Wednesday for 2 hours. Here I would meet not only all the Contra leaders, and Ambassador Otto Reich, but others such as General Wesley Clark and Winston Churchill III would address us. Each week we would be briefed in detail exactly what was happening in Central America. At one such briefing, I met Prudencio Baldedano, which was introduced to the group as a United Pentecostal minister, actually the Spanish equivalent. I was home schooled at the White House in the areas of public policy and humanitarian assistance and domestic and international affairs.

Prudencio Baldedano with ears bandaged.

Nathaniel Urshan was very active working with me in so many of these areas such as the Prudencio Baldedano story in which a Pentecostal preacher in Nicaragua had his ears cut off, his throat cut, tied to a tree and left to die. It is a miracle he survived and was brought to the United States to tell his story. Brother Urshan and the United Pentecostal Church brought his family to the United States and with the help of men, such as Hugh S. Hunt, was given a place to live, found a job, and located in the United States. One of the great pictures in my mind is this man and his family standing in the front of the church with others in Gaithersburg, Maryland, where Ronald Libby pastors, with hands raised praising God, and appeared on the front page above the fold in the *Washington Times*.

Ronald Libby pastored Christian Life Center in Gaithersburg Maryland. He was cooperative and often worked with us in helping to promote the Jesus name message, as well as, the work for the good of the nation. My daughter, Mary Wachtstetter-Harris, worked for Hugh S. Hunt as his executive secretary and as Pastor Libby's part time secretary. My brother, Tim and his wife, worked for both Hugh S. Hunt (lived at his mansion) and worked as Pastor Libby's youth pastors.

Of course, behind all of this, was Nathaniel Urshan working tirelessly in a humanitarian effort to raise money to bring the Baldedano family to the United States. When his family arrived, there were three of us at the Airport to welcome them: Nathaniel Urshan, Robert Sweet –Special Assistant to the President of the United States, and myself. President Reagan formally spoke about this event twice, once at the National Religious Broadcasters Convention and on January 22, 1988 to Civic Leaders at the White House.

In his remarks, the President would say concerning Nathaniel A. Urshan, Ronald Libby, Hugh S. Hunt, and all of those that worked hard on bringing this family to America, "In 1984 Prudencio Baldedano was captured by Sandinista soldiers. His crime? He was an evangelical minister, a Man of God. The soldiers bound him to a tree, beat him, used their bayonets to cut off his ears, and slit his throat. The soldier's commander said he 'wasn't worth wasting a bullet.' 'let him die suffering,' the commander said. As they left him bleeding, the soldier's taunted him saying, 'Pray and see if you're God will save you.'"

"Well, God did save Prudencio Baldedano, and just this last week in Washington, here he was reunited with his wife and six children. You see, a church here in Gaithersburg, Maryland, has sponsored Reverend Baldedano and his family. The church and some other American friends worked to get his wife and children here to the United States from a refugee camp in Costa Rica, to provide them with clothing, and to help them with housing. To me, the help that Mr. Baldedano and his family was given here in the United States, is just an important part of the story as the suffering they endured in Central America. It reminds us that when we see someone in trouble, we Americans reaching out to help. I am delighted that Reverend Baldedano is here with us. Welcome!"

I always enjoyed the speech, that moment, when the President said, "Well, God did save. . .." The President of the United States giving such a national testimony; it reminded me of passages I had read in the Bible of national leaders acknowledging God. The account would not stop here but, where both the struggle to free man from repression and the importance of humanitarian assistance for a better world would be applauded. The President of the United States would next go to the National Religious Broadcasters Convention.

President Reagan was in his element here, as it was a combination of his many years in radio broadcasting, and the evangelical faith that he acquired from his preaching mother. He began his speech rather poetically, "It was in 1921 that the healing words of the Gospel first flew like angels over America's airwaves. Since then, religious broadcasting has been a pillar of radio and television in this nation. This program has helped God's message of salvation enter into millions of homes not just in the United States but in virtually every country of the globe." This was an incredibly strong statement for a President to make. For him to speak in terms of the gospel and of salvation was strong, indeed.

President Reagan saw the battle between good and evil crystal clear and it included everything from salvation, to domestic policy, such as the family and abortion, or international policy as in the Middle East or communism. At NRB he is preaching to the choir and getting rousing amens and applause. NRB is described as the Premier Evangelical Event. It is an event that which Oneness Pentecostals have long been officially shut out. During the Reagan years this event was generally held in Washington, DC, and we had gained acceptance via our friend, Ed McAteer which hosted a Prayer for the Peace of Jerusalem Breakfast each year in conjunction with this event. This is a very nice time when we can relate with both other evangelical groups as well as the nation of Israel. It was then easy to set this time as a gathering of Apostolic leaders in Washington, DC, the White House and to meet with congressional leaders.

I want to take a moment to give a little background, so you understand how important this event was that was about to happen. First, you must understand, the United Pentecostal Church, the Jesus name movement,

Harvesttime Radio broadcast, and Nathaniel and Jean Urshan is an outgrowth of the Jesus name revival that started around 1913 and is an outgrowth of the Pentecostal revival which in turn is an outgrowth of the holiness movement. It was very common to see holiness churches, such as the one pastored by Chisholm in Louisville, Mississippi founded in the 1800s as a holiness church, take part in the Pentecostal revival, and later received a revelation of Jesus name. A. D. Urshan was preaching in the camp meetings in Neshoba county in Mississippi in 1912 - and probably much earlier. You will see the same transformation in the Pentecostal Assemblies of the World. These people always considered themselves to be evangelical, but the vast majority of evangelicals rejected them, first for speaking in tongues, and later for baptism in Jesus name. Later Pentecostalism would tend to be accepted. The United Pentecostal Church always wanted to take their seat at the table with other evangelical groups. What is of interest is that while Pentecostals in general were shut out of the National Association of Evangelicals but were later accepted and became the dominant part of this group. Unfortunately, they were forceful in blocking the apostolic membership in the National Religious Broadcasters up to the date of the writing of this book.

The evangelical movement is far more divided with political games played than it would like outsiders to know. One group is always trying to put down and block another group, to believe in speaking in tongues, baptism in Jesus name, to reject the Trinity, and a life of holiness makes that person or group an easy target of rejection. There are constantly charges of being a cult. I have ministered in the Soviet Union for many years and they grow up being taught that any one that doesn't think like them is a sect. America is far more independent thinking, but groups use this same old foolish talk to exercise their control.

It was here at the National Association of Evangelicals that Brother Urshan would be lauded by all those that had said derogatory remarks about him and his group via President Reagan.

Return to the conflict of good and evil, of the danger of the Evil Empire, and the focus is on the spiritual and political struggle in Central America. He drove this point home by stating, "But there is something more than security at stake: freedom." To Reagan, and many Americans, the issue is the freedom of man, to worship as he feels, to go to church where he wants, to have individual thoughts and not have to state the prescribed line of thinking, and to be able to speak openly. If you think it through, the ultimate in the principle of freedom of thought and expression is religion. If you cannot believe in God as you choose, and worship as you choose, then there is no freedom of thought.

What is about to happen at that meeting will drive home this principle. The National Association of Evangelicals, when formed, carried with it some of the old thinking that originally cut all Pentecostals out, but with broader acceptance may actually hold the majority of the membership of that political body now in parts of Central America. But the same ones that had received rejection themselves, in like manner, could not tolerate not being able to prescribe the exact word usage that a person must use to either baptize or to define God in a certain manner. That is while many areas may be Charismatic or Pentecostal they still block those that baptize in Jesus name, or deny the Trinity, or teach holiness. It is the same intolerance. Every time the President would make a trip to meet with the Soviet, and later Russian Federation leaders, I was invited to share my thoughts with Carolyn Sundseth and this would be factored into his negotiations at whatever meeting. In fact, other groups began to approach me and ask me to advocate for them. I remember one such thought I felt was pertinent and that I shared with Carolyn as a concern of all Apostolic's, and that was the old Soviet had denied Jews the opportunity to learn or speak Hebrew, which was central to their worship. I expressed to her that we considered this very serious, and as I understand, was an issue to which the president spoke directly when he met with the Russians.

To Stan Wachtstetter
With best wishes,

Ronald Reagan.

Stan Wachtstetter
With appreciation and best wishes,

Ronald Reagan

White House Photographer

Constantly, the USSR kept granting more and more freedoms and greater openness as their people were given opportunities to travel West. On November 7, 1982, Brezhnev died and was given a state funeral. George H. W. Bush, Vice President of the United States, was sent as our nation's representative. He later told me that when he saw Mrs. Brezhnev come to the casket and lean over her husband and make the sign of the cross that he knew communism would collapse. He thought to himself that if they could not keep religion out of the General Secretary's house how could they keep it out anywhere in Russia.

The new General Secretary Mikhail Gorbachev would surprise us all by talking about greater openness, and during a visit to Washington DC would actually get out of his car and walk down the street shaking hands with average Americans. His intention in doing this is to show them they had nothing to fear. Many blamed him, and many credit him, but it appeared the USSR had little choice at that time. Constantly they were falling further and further behind the United States economically. There were so many reasons for this but one key one is always in a totalitarian state you have the inability to share information and with the advent of the computer we were leaping further and further ahead while in cumbersome manner they were lagging behind.

Mikhail Gorbachev would be the last of the General Secretaries, and the last President of the USSR. Greater and greater freedoms are being permitted, the economy in Russia kept falling, and United States of America continued to put pressure bringing about the eventual collapse of the Soviet Union. In 1988, I was invited to a very special meeting in the East room of the White House celebrating "The Millennial of Russia being a Christian Nation." This of course is a little bit of a rewriting of history as has been done by the Rus. In fact, we can see from Pentecost in Jerusalem when the church was started that there was Christian activity in this region from this time on till this day. The celebration is more about the restructuring of the society in that region to proclaim the Rus as the founders and beginners of the entire region. Prince Vladimir, a Kyevian Rus, was baptized and this was the beginning of the Orthodox Church in that region. The occasion was a little humorous as the various speakers got up from the different church groups with the first being the Russian Orthodox stating that 1,000 years ago Russian Orthodox Church began, and the second being from the Ukrainian Orthodox Church stating that no the Russian Orthodox church had not been established until much later with the beginning of Ukrainian Orthodox Church. They went back and forth on this and I was just thankful that they weren't Pentecostal speakers. A meeting such as this was to put pressure on the Soviet Union by reminding of the lack of religious freedom in that country, and that its history had been one of strong faith.

Nathaniel Urshan died never having really received the appreciation from the United States that he deserved. This was in part because there was no direct linkage between the church and the government in these activities. Like the book of Esther, the King and the Queen, dwelt in separate houses. It is, likely, that because of this wall of separation that Reagan could never completely reveal the part Urshan had played.

It is clear, the President of the United States, did in fact, appreciate all General Superintendent Urshan had sacrificed for the good of mankind. This is reflected in the times he openly showed it at the White House and at the

National Religious Broadcasters Convention. It is emphasized in a video that the White House specially made to be shown at the 64th annual convention of the United Pentecostal Church. But this was a very special event that was approved at the highest levels, and is in fact, a very rare event. The following are the words the President used.

"It is a wonderful opportunity for me to address you at your 64th annual conference and join you in prayer for God's blessing upon our great nation, may all of us continue to strive to keep America free and at peace.

"The Bible is a wellspring of wisdom and guidance for all, and I know the central role it plays in all your deliberations and worship at this conference. The Bible stresses the importance of family prayer, family participation in the house of God, and family unity. The family that works together as a harmonious unit shows the world, 'that the family prays together stays together.'

"As president I have attempted to restore prayer in our public schools it is of the utmost importance that the church continues to espouse this cause. The day a nation does not nourish its children on spiritual things, is the day that nation begins its decline. Prayer is a basic for strength and spiritual power without it we become weak and misdirected.

"It's also refreshing for me to know that the good people of the United Pentecostal church are assisting in the struggle against abortion. You are taking a strong stand to protect the right to life of the unborn.

"It was also through the efforts of the United Pentecostal church and others that the Siberian Seven were given the privilege of coming to freedom and this country. We must not stop our effort to seek freedom for other Pentecostal believers in the Soviet Union and for all those under oppression.

"Your kind of courageous loyalty to the cause of human rights has helped at every turn. But thanks to the United Pentecostal church for Prudencio Baldedano had the opportunity to be a free man to pursue his ministry without fear of death or mistreatment.

"I count the eight years that I spent as President of the United States to have been a great privilege, but the best days are ahead for this great country if we continue to work together.

"May each of you fulfill your call as a preacher of the Gospel. May you continue to express your compassion for the down trodden and forgotten, and may you inspire effort in promoting religious liberty in all countries for all people bear fruit."

"With best wishes to General Superintendent Nathaniel A. Urshan, and General Secretary Cleveland M. Becton, to all the officials, leaders, pastors, and ministers, Nancy and I send our respect and love. Thank you. God bless you."

Of note, because it was rather personal and to the church and especially a great church leader, absent is the usual ending, "and God bless the United States of America". In this speech, the President of United States, acknowledges the great humanitarian work done by a religious group such as the United Pentecostal church, but in reality, he Is speaking to the great work of Nathaniel Urshan. This man, used of God, opened the door to a massive part of the world (17%) to hear the gospel and have it preached openly. He had been involved in the beginning, likely unwittingly, and the first domino to free the Siberian Seven, and had been used periodically over the years to help people all over the world which included those in central and South America, and by doing so ended the evil empire

Brother Urshan and Apostolic leaders leaving a briefing at the White House.

General Superintendent Urshan would work tirelessly for the good of the countries of the old Soviet Union. There would be conferences, large groups of American pastors visiting that region with him, sponsoring the churches, distribution of bibles, renting equipment and tracks, and missionaries in almost every country. He felt a keen sense of responsibility for this region.

This meant the Urshan family and the Apostolic's had been involved with Eastern Europe from before the start of the communist revolution, across the Soviet Era, and was still there and active in the rusting away of the Iron Curtain.

I'm reminded of an incident years later in which I would be honored by the Mayor's Office of Saint Petersburg, Russia and I would be taken to a podium where I was told Lenin had spoken to the Bolsheviks, and I asked, "May I say something and take pictures?" And they said, "Yes, that's why we brought you here," and I began to quote Acts 2: 38. It was my celebration that after 70 years of heavy persecution the gospels still stood in the world.

At the end of the taped speech, the President addressed the General Superintendent Urshan with special remarks, but it was in fact Urshan himself that had guided this church group to accomplish humanitarian efforts all over the world that drew international attention.

Stanley Wachtstetter, Bishop Worthy Rowe, Bishop R. Little, Vice President George Bush, Don Johnson, James Larson, N. A. Urshan, Bishop Isaac Coda meeting at the Vice Presidents home for the first time.

United Pentecostal Church, Int. General Superintendent
Nathaniel A. Urshan.

## Chapter Six

## Stanley Earl Wachtstetter

## And

## God's Open Door

This is the period in which I began to minister in Russia, which was an outgrowth of the work that I had been doing in Washington DC. It was God's blessing on my life that during this period I met almost every major political figure both Republican and Democrat, and every significant religious figure in the popular press. One of those key figures that really helped me along the way was a man by the name of Ed McAteer and his Religious Roundtable. Ed is one of the least appreciated but most significant of the religious right, and he had greater influence and was able to accomplish more than almost anyone else. He and James Robinson had hosted The National Affairs Briefing that was held in Dallas, Texas, that had springboard Ronald Reagan in the front runner among conservatives.

Ed hosted an event every year at the National Religious Broadcasters Convention that was called the Prayer for the Peace of Jerusalem Prayer Breakfast. This was basically a pro-Israel Christian group and he actively invited me to participate and treated myself and other Apostolics with great fairness. The speakers were awesome and powerful.

One of my great memories was sitting on the dais and as providence would have it, I was situated in the middle on the third row, with George W. Bush, and George H. W. Bush, the 41st president of the United States and then vice president on the center front row. Now, the fun was neither of the Bushes', father or son knew many of the other ministers, but they did know me and so there was a lot of just posturing and talking and I was able to spend several minutes with them. Obviously, I spent more time with George W. Bush at this event than with his father.

My high status with the presidents had made me very popular with the NRB and particularly Ben Armstrong and we became very good friends. There were constantly other meetings growing out of these connections and one such meeting had to do with the translation of a modern-day Bible called **God's Word.** I was invited to be part of a consultant committee on this translation and was able to get several of our ministers involved, including Nathaniel Urshan, James Kilgore, and Pastor Lyles. A committee meeting was held in the Dallas-Fort Worth area to which we all attended. At this meeting, Ben Armstrong came to me and said he was going to Russia to begin opening state radio and television for Christian broadcasting and invited me to go. This was 1989 and the Communists were still in control in the Gorbachev era.

When Ed came to me I was very excited and interested in making this trip, but what I did not realize was that it was perhaps more of a tourist trip than anything else and was being promoted by Lavon Riley, a popular evangelical tour company owner. I immediately told him I wanted to make the trip to Russia and began laying plans. I was told if I could get three other pastors to go on the trip and pay their own way that my trip would be paid. I immediately began to contact a few ministers and Bishop Worthy Rowe, of the Apostolic World Christian Fellowship, indicated he was interested in making that trip. I was not able to get everything together, so I was not able to make that first trip in early 1989 but Bishop Rowe went ahead and went on the trip. He visited Russia and the Ukraine and did some teaching in a university at Kiev. As such, he is the first formal Apostolic American to go to Russia and the Soviet Union with the purpose of preaching the gospel.

Shortly thereafter, I was contacted by Lavon Riley again and told that all I needed was two other ministers to go and my way would be free. I made a few calls and Anthony Mansfield of Meridian, Mississippi, and Bishop Alfonso Brooks of Washington, DC were both eager to go with me. This meant my way was free, and God seemed to be in it and blessing. Because the earlier group had covered more cities their cost was higher and there was a little money differential that was to be passed on to me. In addition, Lavon was unable to make the trip and he asked that I serve as the host and therefore I was given additional money. I mentioned this, because for my first few trips I paid nothing to be able to go and God worked great financial miracles. It seemed the Holy Ghost was pushing me in this direction. In fact, God worked great miracles on my first four missionary journeys into the old Soviet Union so that I did not have to pay airfare for any of these trips.

This seemed to me to be a significant sign from God that he was sending me.

If I was going to make this long journey into an area of uncertainty and hardship, then I wanted it to be a blessing to the people of God there, and something that would count for Christ. I began to search and to study, and I called all around looking for an apostolic contact for someone that I could start with in the Soviet Union. I finally discovered one name, a Sister Irina and her mother, Marie. These folks lived in Moscow and through a third-party they had been referred to me as solid Jesus name Pentecostal people. You must remember the door had been closed for 70 years, and even the people there were not permitted to travel or get together, and thus it was impossible to tell who was or was not Bible believing. It would take me four years traveling the country to dig out believers, and congregations in different parts of Russia.

As it turned out Sister Irina was a wonderful contact and full of information. Her mother had been a high official, in the Kremlin, as a chief economist in the Khrushchev and Brezhnev years. They had both given their hearts to the Lord and were strong believers. They were attending what many would term "an Ushant church" in Moscow. Later Sister Irina would become the official translator for the United Pentecostal Church and before missionaries were sent she would serve as the key contact person for that organization, Later, she would marry Brother Ernie Dumeresque of the St. Louis area where he would pastor and reside, and she would work with United Pentecostal Church at their headquarters.

I was all set to go on my first journey when I began to explore the possibility of finding Bibles printed in Russian that I could carry to give to the churches. I located a source that would only cost me five dollars a book and they were about one half a pound each. At the last moment, someone put me in contact with Pastor Butler in Wisconsin and he had a member in his church that had a burden for just such a need. I was supplied with 500 Bibles and was excited but had not thought it through as this was 250 pounds. It was exhausting but Anthony Mansfield, Bishop Alphonso Brooks and I shared this load and carried these Bibles through to the then Soviet Union – USSR. Technically this was illegal, but no one seemed to mind.

I remember distinctly my first visit arriving in the Moscow airport with its great concrete walls and soldiers in military uniform with automatic weapons and the lighting so dim it seemed lost in the walls. Remember this was before 9/11, and by contrast our airports were wide open, colorful, with bright lights and a sense of welcoming us. After touring the city, the three of us ministers met with Sister Irina at the hotel. People from America had sent many gifts and we blessed her with Bibles, gifts, and money. She in turn had been a great help and provided me with the name and phone number of Dmitry Shatrov in Leningrad. Over the 25 years I ministered thus far in the old Soviet Union, it was my great joy that God used me to be able to carry Bibles, gifts of many kinds, and money to help individuals and churches. There is a great joy in giving, and I learned and taught the message of the "Loaves and Fishes." The lesson of the loaves and fishes is that God multiplies what is given. I had not taken from any missionary group and only one or two local churches funded us for a year or more at very small offerings- never more than a hundred dollars a month. God blessed, and I was able to do so much with so little. I never worried about an IRS audit because there was way more given out than was donated. You might ask how, and it would be the miraculous power of God.

I remember to this day the inconveniences of Moscow in those early days, staying in what they considered a four-star hotel. I joked that the mattress on the bed was thinner than the steak I ate when I got back to the Old New York Steakhouse as a guest of Herb Zwiebon, with the **Americans for a Safe Israel**. In Moscow I was tired, exhausted and slept solid and on awakening my muscles locked up in my joints unable to move. My dear friend, Pastor Anthony Mansfield, declared he would never share a room with me again because of my incredibly loud snoring. He remains my close buddy.

In Leningrad we would find the core of our ministry on this first mission into the USSR. Not knowing the phone system numbers or anything else our guide helped me in locating Dmitry Shatrov and we invited him to have dinner with us at the hotel. Now the cost of the meals was so incredibly cheap, 10 rubles for breakfast, 15 rubles for lunch, and 25 rubles for dinner and I could get 40 rubles to the dollar on the black market. The economy was in shambles and prices were all over the place. It was clear that the Iron Curtain had rusted away leaving the people without food or money. Pastor Shatrov invited us to his flat for dinner and invited us to preach in his church. I was so tired that I was inclined to say why don't you just come over and have dinner with us at the hotel, I will be happy to buy your meal, but the Holy Ghost checked me, and I said that we accepted his invitation.

Here I was going to begin to learn many things about Russia that would be hard for an American to understand without having the experience. The table was filled with food and jokingly I said, "I see there is no shortage of food in Leningrad. The pastor rebuked me by telling me that that day every woman in the church had gone out and stood in long lines for each of them to get small amounts of delicacies to fill the table. As I sat at the table I noticed that the padded bench on which I sat with my back against the wall was much wider than I was used to it being, and then I realized it was designed to be also a bed. Someone slept here at night as their dwellings were too small to have private bedrooms, and each room doubled. I would see this many times in the future with large numbers compressed in what we would consider a small living space. It was, nevertheless, a warm, comfortable abode.

I would learn, that while they were not used to the comforts and lifestyle I enjoyed, that communism had provided the masses with warmth, a roof over their head, and an education. That Russians had far more than the average person in the world. I'm not saying this to glorify the system, nor was it all it should be, but I did understand why the masses realized they had more than the serfs of the past. Sister Shatrov had worked hard to provide a comfortable home and a pleasant meal for us.

In the church and in the home, the presentations were with a great deal of formality. This was something of which, as an American, I was not expecting. I remember in the church that I said, "I bring you greetings from America." When I said this everyone in the church stood straight up and it caused a bit of noise that confused me and stopped me for a moment. They were receiving a formal greeting and responding accordingly to it. In his home, the pastor made a formal presentation of himself and his family. The way this was done was backwards for an American; he said that he was of the family – Shatrov, and that his name was Dmitri. I would've simply said that I was Stanley Wachtstetter. I later learned that there was a mental thought process that divided us far more than the surface context here. That when they address a letter they put their nation first, then their city or district, then their street address, then the family name, and finally their given name. This is the reverse of the way we would address a letter, and it has deep meaning as in our society the individual is the important thing, then the family in which he dwells, then his address, then his city and state and finally nation. We think of ourselves as the most important in the center, but they have been taught to think collectively with the state being the most important.

In the Soviet years, the average person had never dined in a restaurant nor stayed in a hotel, and if they did this, it would have been for some very exceptional reason such as a honeymoon or major event. Dining in the home was an art. There was both a process to the serving of the food and the importance of a great assortment of food that took me some time to learn. I remember cakes and desserts being set out and I went to take a piece, but someone said that they would not eat until the desert plates were brought out. I would learn the variety of Russian salads that were so excellent, and the various meats. In early 1990, few Soviets had ever met an American and this was a big deal. On one of my trips I remember a person coming up to me on the street, someone I've never met, and said if you will come to my apartment I will throw a great feast and invite all my friends. In those days, they were quite curious about us and over the next few years, they would come to love and respect us, until these last few years where things have changed, and Americans are greatly disliked.

So, this was my first visit at a Russian home and it was such a wonderful evening. We talked, we ate, we laughed, and I met the whole family. It was as enjoyable as my first visit to his church. The church was a little different and colder than I was used to which I attributed to the January weather. It was more formal than I was used to in relaxed America.

There was a desk, a large wooden desk, like you might've seen in a school room, sitting up next to the pulpit and behind it sat the pastor. There was a pulpit and I spoke from it. The congregation seemed stiff by what I was used to, but this was our first meeting and I expected a certain amount of nervousness. I tried not to say anything that might be interpreted politically controversial. I learned this stiffness was in fact the routine nature of their church service and they did not practice open worship as we might see in American. This, then was a great contrast, as Americans by any other nationality might be seen as far more outgoing than the norm.

We had a wonderful evening and enjoyed ourselves very much. I asked them to meet with me the next day to discuss future plans for Russia. Now my income that year was about $10,000 and I was pastoring a very small church. I was below the poverty line and had very little money to work with and no real promise of being able to raise anything. I could feel the presence of God telling me to help, and I determined by faith to do what God would provide. This was reinforced by a testimony Lady Shatrova shared with me. Our first meeting in a Russian's home was the Shatrov's home. When we got there and went through many of the formalities Lady Shatrova said in English," May I tell you a mystery?" I realized this was broken English and found the phrase fascinating but said that I wanted to hear. She began to tell me that when she was a young girl a prophecy had been given over her that when Americans visited in her flat in Leningrad, the door between the East and the West would be open and communism would collapse for a time and then the door would close again. Here we had been at her apartment the first Americans to ever visit in her flat.

She said that everyone had laughed because the prophecies seemed so absurd as she lived in Estonia and had no hope of ever living in Leningrad. Christians were barred from living within 100 km of Moscow or Leningrad. She was a little girl and the idea that Americans would visit her was as strange as the wise men coming to see Jesus. Yet, all of this would come true. That summer the Soviet Union would collapse. Now in all fairness as I reported this event, somehow, I never heard her say the door would shut again, but all the Russians there say it was said and I accept it.

Anthony Mansfield and Stanley Wachtstetter, Americans eating dinner in St. Petersburg at the Shatrov's apartment. What an honor to be with them! Brother Shatrov is the man sitting at the left lower corner.

Eating in Sister Shatrov's apartment fulfilled the prophecy and she was confident that Communism was going to fall.

Sister Shatrov and S. E. Wachtstetter getting ready to hand out Bibles donated by U. S. Apostolic churches.

All the churches present at the conference received Bibles.

Already feeling the direction of the Holy Ghost to go forward and to help Russia and hearing this testimony I asked the pastor to help me create a list of things we could do to get started. He said I don't know how big to ask, I told him that I had no money so if he needed $1,000 I did not have it, if he needed $10,000 I did not have it, and if he needed $100,000 I did not have it. I told him whatever we did God was going to have to provide, so that he might as well ask for $100,000 as $1,000-God was going to have to do it. What God was going to do over the next 25 years was so much more than the numbers we were talking about that even I find it hard to believe, as I sit here and write this now, and it is marvelous in our sight. It would be at least millions of dollars that I would see God provide.

Dmitry started with the usual list of Bibles, printed materials, a printing press, and money. I assured him we would go to work on this and try to raise what was needed. Then he told me that what he really needed was a conference. That other church groups were starting to have conferences and that their need was to be able to bring their group together in a conference.  Remember that during the Soviet years you had to have a visa to travel from city to city and these were routinely denied to church members. Thus, they had never been able to have a really large convocation, or the exchange of ideas and doctrinal views. They were much like our long-horned cattle out on the range in which the rancher had no idea how many he really had until they were rounded up. To make their organization function they needed a large gathering where they could meet and begin to function as a body. They were somewhat limited in their vision for outreach, but I was thinking in terms of a mass gathering in which new people could be introduced to the truth. We had some contention on this matter when I suggested we run an ad in the paper inviting anyone to attend. I learned just how desperate the situation was when he explained to me that this was going to be a wonderful event and why should we share it with those added who never accepted the gospel when sincerely hungry hearts that had stood through persecution would want to be in that chair. I told him we will get a bigger building, and he told me you give me however large a number you want of faithful saints.

Brother Haney once said to me, "We really blew it when the door to Russia first opened that we did not rush in with everything we had." Of course, I was thinking you were still missing the boat. What was laid out before me was something that by today's standards was so ridiculously simple and inexpensive that who can tell what we might've accomplished if we repeated this all over the Soviet Union. Bro. Shatrov told me that it would cost $6,000 to get the largest meeting place in the city and be able to host 10 ministers from America as well at the meeting place. With the small amount of money, we would be able to have an incredibly large conference, have meals, and provide some form of adequate housing for the pastors coming in from Russia, and those from the USA. This was an exciting idea, but you would be shocked at how little money I had and the prospects-doing this seemed difficult.

On my way home, on the airplane, God began to deal with me and I started thinking a little larger. I began to think if I could get 20 ministers, a group rate on the airplane of about $700 round-trip and asked each of them to donate $300 with $200 of it being for their care, and $100 being for the conference. This would net $6,000 and I would push Bishop Shatrov to provide the additional housing. I could begin to see this as a real possibility.

When I got home, God had a big surprise for me, because God was motivating what I was doing He had already provided more than I needed even though I was unaware. I remember I was very jetlagged, and I had begun to call around to tell various people about this opportunity and they were showing interest. I received a phone call from Pastor Butler in Wisconsin asking about how the trip had gone, and the Bibles that had been donated. When I gave him the report he said," Mike is going to want to hear this." Shortly thereafter, I received a phone call from the office of Michael Polaski indicating he wanted to make a sizable donation, and that he was very interested in what I was doing. Now, I know many, many wealthy people and seldom do they actually part with money of real significance so I was a little skeptical, and I said fine, get an airplane ticket, fly me up, and we'll talk. Within an hour, I received a phone call from Mike's secretary. She notified me there was an E ticket waiting for me at the airport to fly out immediately, the hotel had been arranged, and that she would meet me at the airport. I remember I flew Midwest air in which every seat was first class and they baked cookies on the plane. Now, I could not help but notice that God was doing something very special.

Mike Polaski was a high-energy man that was excited about the Holy Ghost and the things of God, and desired to bring his business knowledge to the spread of the gospel. He was one of the finest people I've ever met. Later there would be a wedge driven between us, and I always felt bad about that, but there was nothing I could do. I had to accept that God had brought him into my life for this moment, and I could see that he was going to be used to help the kingdom of God in Russia without me, and in that I celebrated and thanked God for His kingdom going forward. As I explained to Mike what I had seen in Russia and the potential he became excited and began to speak of the "Winds of Change", which became the theme of the conference. Wonderful words were spoken to me, "I will pay for everything," he said. There and then the budget was increased.

Remember, most of these Russian pastors have never had the opportunity for travel, some had never seen Leningrad/St. Petersburg, most had never stayed in a hotel, many had never eaten at a nice restaurant, and above all they had not had the opportunity to fellowship with their fellow apostolics. I have always praised God that I had been blessed to be able to bring about this event that was going to inspire so many. It was arranged for all of us to stay at the Prebaltiskya Hotel, with meeting rooms in the daytime for gatherings in the hundreds, meals served in their outstanding restaurant for the whole group, monies provided to bring pastors and church leaders in from all over the Soviet Union, and the famous October Concert Hall was the site of the great convocation seating 4,500 people.

There is a phrase at the end of the book of Mark, "the Holy Ghost working with them." If that statement was ever true it was true in the miracle of what would take place in Leningrad.

The great miracle was not in the provision of money, although that was needed and wonderful, but the real miracle was in the prophecy related by Lady Shatrov. In January, she had related what God had given in prophecy over her, and in August Rev. Don Johnson and I were to carry a few thousand dollars over to make arrangements for this meeting. To our amazement, the very week that we were to carry the money there was a standoff in Yeltsin's government and Yelsti-won and it was the collapse of the Soviet Union. My wife Helen called Sister Shatrov to show concern and ask if she was all right, and she replied, "Yes, of course, this is the fulfillment of the prophecy." We cancelled our flight and rescheduled the next week. In January, we had selected a date for the conference and everything had been arranged, not knowing what would happen, but the exact date we had selected for this event in the October Concert Hall was the date that officially all the names of the city's that had communist names were changed, and as such it was the day that Leningrad became St. Petersburg. This was termed the re-baptism of Russia, and we had all the best places nailed down. Others wanted to come in and do things, but God had given us the preeminence.

We cancelled the trip and rebooked it the next week. Fortunately, they were first class tickets. God had blessed, and I did not have to pay for tickets for my first four mission trips to the old Soviet Union. To me, this was the blessing of God. I had contacted Finnair and explained to them I was going to try to create groups going to Russia and was going to be on a site inspection. They provided me with two free first-class tickets. I invited my General Superintendent, of the Assemblies of the Lord Jesus Christ, Don Johnson, to go with me. On this trip, I carried $6,000 with me and had previously had a brother Poe carry $5,000 that was given to brother Shatrov. God Blessed and we were able to provide much more than the original request.

While we were there we were hosted by Sister Irina and her mother. One of the humorous stories, that was quite serious, that reflects the conditions of the time was that we were staying in the apartment owned by Irina and her mother. They would cook for us, provide us a meeting place, showed us around the city and in general cared for us. But at night they would leave the apartment and go to stay with a cousin. When sister Irina got ready to leave she very seriously said to us, "Everything is legal, and you have the right to be here. But if anyone knocks on the door do not open it until we return and unlock the door in the morning". She explained that people might pretend to be the police or something and say we are illegal and demand some money. Then she became very agitated and said, "Please, whatever you do, do NOT open the door". I said, "ok", but she was almost frantic and said again, "Please, please do NOT open the door". She left the apartment and locked the door and Bro. Johnson and I were all alone. I had not told Bro. Johnson so as not to alarm him and make him nervous. I went to bed and just as I was dozing off, I could hear someone was knocking on the door. I breathed a silent prayer, "OH! God! please don't let Brother Johnson open that door." In the morning, I asked Brother Johnson about it and he said he did not hear it.

I met with Dmetry and Victor Shatrov and worked out all the details of the Conference. I explained that we had an additional $6,000 to work with and this money was for the purpose to provide funding to bring in pastors and church workers from all over the Soviet Union to provide for their hotel stay and banquets. Most of these pastors had never had the luxury of staying in a hotel or dining in a restaurant. We were going to provide them with a truly outstanding conference.

While we were in Moscow, Brother Johnson and I had the privilege of preaching at a church that Irina and her mother attended. It was an old Urshanite church that met in a school, so we had the opportunity to see what a Russian school looked like, as well as minister in a local Russia Apostolic church service. We attended the church and had a private meeting with the pastor, and for us as Americans, it was rather sad. It was very stiff and quiet with about 100 in attendance with the men in the front and the women in the back and when the people prayed you could hear a sort of hum. I noticed that the women especially cupped their hands over their mouth as they prayed. The differences were so great, and we tolerated them as they tolerated us. I had real patience with them as I realized they had suffered so much. In the meeting with the pastor he pulled out the pictures of all the pastors that had served over the years going all the way back to Urshan and Somordin. He would point to one and say he had died in prison, then point to the next one and say he died in prison. They had had a great meeting house that had been taken from them by the communists and they were hoping we could get it back for them. Later, I learned of a great service provided by that church of a soup kitchen and help for orphans. They had suffered so much over the years and their pastors all died while serving as pastor and died in prison. This to me was the persecuted church and all you could do was love them.

Tartarstan mission trip visiting Red Square. Jon Wachtstetter Irina Wachtstetter, Kristina Sadovnikova, Stan Wachtstetter, Lynna McMillan, Mary Wachtstetter Harris, Sandra Gonzalis, Amelia Burmudez, Helen Wachtstetter, John Hancock

As it turned out, on our next trip, there were about 40 Americans in the entire group, which was more than the original 20 I had hoped. Most of these had donated an additional $200 that would be given to the church, and because Mike was paying for everything; this permitted us to give this rather nice offering to Pastor Shatrov for the work of God. This would be a small amount of the overall blessing that would be raised from the United States to help with the work of God in that region.

For the conference, Mark and Lori Carouthers, were selected to be the music leaders. They were, at the time, the music ministers at Calvary Tabernacle in Indianapolis with Pastor Paul D. Mooney. Also, Rev. James McFall, the author of "Thank God I'm Free", provided the theme song and sang it more than once at the events that took place. We held services at the church, the hotel, and with the major event at the October Concert Hall. We had thousands of tracks that were distributed on every seat in the meetings, and we had American and Russian preachers taking turns. God had blessed, and Brother Urshan provided 10,000 Bibles to be distributed to the 200 churches participating in this event. This was an average of 50 Bibles to a church and the beginning of tens of thousands of Bibles that God would bless me to be able to distribute across Russia.

There were constantly the abrasions of the differences in worship style, administration, and doctrinal views between the nations involved. To add to this problem, was the popularity of Americans at that time in the eyes of the

Russian church members, which only irritated our Russian brothers even more. Newcomers often see our way of worship as a concert style and would stand on benches, gyrate, and simply have a very good time which was so incredibly sacrilegious to the rather stiff Russians. Despite all this, there was a commonality and a working relationship between all of us. At the end, we had a great banquet-very formal in a beautiful dining Hall-something I found to be so wonderful to be able to have for these that had suffered so many decades under the tyranny of deprivation. Dmitry Shatrov said, "The week had made us like rocks in a stream where we had rubbed each other and struck each other and finally refined and smoothed one another."

Because of this conference churches all across the Old Soviet Union were strengthened and encouraged and had materials to use. At our meetings, everyplace would be full, every seat was filled in the October Concert Hall and they turned people away, in the church meetings there would be special boards put out across aisles so that there were more seats, every seat was taken from the front to the back and my daughter was brought in and squeezed in between the Russians in between the isles up front and my wife which came a little late found a special spot reserved for her in a closet. When the altar calls were given, there were so many that crowded in, it was impossible to count them all, but so very many responded. As a result, the church in St. Petersburg was in the hundreds after this meeting.

I returned to America with great jubilation. This had been my third missionary trip to Russia and I had never seen myself as a missionary, and therefore was prepared to settle down, pastor my church, and try to influence the public policy of Mississippi and the United States. It seemed that I had God's special blessing on what I was doing; it was as the kiss of God's approval. When I made my second missionary journey, the day before I left, my wife and I attended a State Dinner at the White House. Certainly, to be invited was one of the highest honors of my life in the civil world. Following my third missionary journey, I was invited to give a prayer at a banquet with the Republican Party of Mississippi and a variety of candidates for governor. There, I met Kirk Fordice for the first time. A day later, he came by my office and we prayed together, and I gave him one of the Bibles in Russian that we had passed out. He would become governor and on one occasion he publicly said that without Stan he would not be governor and went on to rehearse how he had been nowhere in the polls but stopped by my office and we had prayed. He gave honor to God and prayer for that election.

I now found myself very busy as I had been given a very nice position in the Governor's Office for Literacy, had a wonderful church to pastor, and was appointed a White House Commissioner. But God was not to leave me alone in this area, as there were so very few that had really responded to the call of evangelizing the Old Soviet Union. I found myself somewhat of an expert on the subject.

A Doctor contacted me wanting to know if I could help him get a Russian Bible. Of course, I gladly provided him with one but when I ask why he wanted it, he told me there were Russian exchange doctors at the Mississippi University Hospital and that a wife of one of the doctors wanted a Bible to read. He introduced her to me and they became friends of our family and started attending our church and soon I found this to be not only international missions, but a local issue. The local newspaper did an interview which gave attention to the church and caused others to want to work with us. The Jackson State college was heavily into exchange programs with Russia. We were invited to help in this and we met the exchange Professors and invited them to Church they and each group that came after that would tell the next group to get in touch with us. We would visit them and invite them to church. Several received the Holy Ghost and were baptized in Jesus name. Next, we were invited to meet the new exchange high school students. These students needed homes to stay in for the school year. Our task was to help find homes. We approached our church family and any apostolic family in the state. We were able to place many of the students in Apostolic homes who had never been to church in their lives. We had about four families in our church participate. As well as several of our churches in other cities. Our church families each took four boys the first year and four girls the second year. Most received the Holy Ghost and were baptized in Jesus name. We had our own mission field right there in Clinton, Mississippi. We were able to keep track of them across the state and hear of their progress in finding the Lord Jesus

Christ. We were able to visit our exchange student in Moscow on one of our mission trips to Russia. And a few of our exchange students and professors came to our conference in Tartarstan. It was difficult at first for the students and professors because there were no churches for them to go to when they got home. But praise God the churches soon came.

Young Dmitri Shatrov asked if we could help put together a trip around the United States to help them raise funds for the church in Russia. I told them we would try our best to help with this, but that I was personally very busy and would not be able to go with them. It was arranged that my precious wife who did so much for Russia but has been given so very little credit and almost no appreciation, went to work scheduling, and that my son would drive them around the nation to the various church meetings. This was

St. Petersburg Youth Choir and Dorma instruments playing during the Conference.

Dmitry Shatrov with young Russian singers from the College touring the U. S. to raise funds for medical supplies for St. Petersburg in exchange for a building for their church. Jon Wachtstetter in tennis shoes drove their bus. Bro. and Sis Wachtstetter and Mary also in the picture in front of their church in Clinton, MS. which attracted Mrs. Fordice to the project.

Dmitri's first visit to the United States and would introduce him from which he would later have many many contacts and is still raising money to this date by God's blessing. Dmitri is a visionary and, even in his youth, a man of great faith. There was, in Leningrad, an unfinished movie theater, and in those days because of the shortage of money, many buildings sitting around would be given by the government if you could just finish them. As he walked by and begin to pray he felt impressed to go ask the city government for that building, and they said no. This building was four stories, extremely large with various auditoriums and located next to the Metro system. Dmitry felt that if they could finish the building they could lease out shops, and have apartments for visiting ministers, and auditoriums for worship. After communism collapsed he went back and asked if it were possible to have this building to finish out. On this occasion the city said yes, if you can get Americans to contribute half million dollars in medical supplies. They were desperate for just basic medical supplies. They needed basic things like aspirin. I myself had carried Band-Aids and sutures for hospitals to use. I'd become friends with doctors at University Medical Center. We were especially close with two Russian doctors, Dr. Zubkov, and Dr. Beneshivlli. These doctors were very close and helped us in many ways and occasionally visited the church. In fact, a wing at the University Medical Center was named after Dr. Alexander Zubkov. Later, when transferring medical supplies to the city of St. Petersburg these men would sleep on the floor of my church office while sending faxes back and forth to that city's Mayors office because of the vast difference in time between both countries. These were exciting days.

Support from American pastors such as JD and Billey Shoulders in Nashville and Bishop Samuel Valverde of the

Apostolic Assemby in California and Bishop Peter Rowe of Indiana to name of few who made this work possible. So many others should be named as supporters, but God knows who you are and God Bless you! The support crosses all Apostolic groups and we are grateful.

Governor Fordice's wife Pat Fordice and Helen Wachtstetter with Dr. Subkov and Dr. Beneshevely recognized for helping to get Medical supplies to St. Petersburg.

The secret to raising funds is involving the right people. You must know the people for the task that you want to accomplish. Many times, the work we do for the good of people is not simply evangelism. In the case of humanitarian assistance, there are so very many that you can link with that may be not doctrinally aligned with you. When it comes to dealing with the church you want to be very doctrinaire, but in providing medical supplies you can broaden your vision to those outside the church, or even believers. The day came when I was visiting with the First Lady of Mississippi, Pat Fordice, and I told her about this project and she became very excited. She offered her help and began to form a group called "Mississippians Reaching Out". This group more than raised the half million that was needed and in fact, raised millions in medical supplies for that city.

Helen was prepared for our ministry in Russia at a young age in Montesano, Washington. There was a family in her church as she was growing up in the fifties who were immigrants from Russia. The Lukens would get up in service every time there were testimonies and sing "At the Cross" in Russian, and then ask for prayer for their brothers and sisters in Russia. The first trip to Russia we were walking into the church which was in progress and they were standing singing "At the Cross" in Russian which she recognized immediately. Helen burst into tears as she realized their prayers were being answered after all these years by God sending us to that country.

To go, and to minister internationally to people outside of your comfort zone; you need a love and a burden for those people together with a miracle working God. I found the Russian people to be at their core, as individuals, to be a sweet and wonderful people. They were not used to our ways and we are not used to theirs. Much of the differences are far more about money than anything else. When you are poor many of the things you do seems odd. Cover this with pride and insecurity and you have what seems like a hostile group but cut through all of this and you find that people are just people. I spent many years trying my best to get needed help to a variety of groups of people. At the core, I wanted to bless and help the Apostolic Church, and this meant preaching, teaching, conferences, church services, Bibles, literature, buses and vans, church buildings, and other needed supplies. To do this work we were called on to help orphans and widows, to help with camp's, and to provide patterns that others would follow later.

Bishop Stan Wachtstetter

Preaching in St. Petersburg Church.

Red Square handing out Bibles.

Jon Wachtstetter walking through a group of Red Army soldiers in Moscow. He was an exchange student in Volgograd and studied for a year than lived off and on in Russia between renewing his visa in a timely fashion. Jon passed away in 2015 after a tour in the army. He was a great asset to our ministry and is greatly missed!

There were so many that became involved and helped, over the years, that I would fail to mention them all. Many including myself wondered why God had called me to Mississippi just when I was gaining incredible prominence in Washington DC. God knew the future and he placed me in a perfect position, where the co-chairs of the Republican Party would be located, a governor that would be close to me, and many high officials ready to help. Add to this a large number of apostolic believers in the state. District Superintendent G. R. Travis and Rev. James Nation would be a significant help with the United Pentecostal Church. Here was a camp meeting that was attended by almost every high official in the state and the politicos were friendly to the church. Of course, there was Rev. Raymond Bishop and Rev. Steve Wilson that had both been general superintendents of the Assemblies of the Lord Jesus Christ, and Bishop Clifton Jones of the Pentecostal Assemblies of the World. All these would lift their support and help in the task that God had given me.

A significant and key person, Ruth Ann Williams, which I met first in Washington D. C. when she was running for Congress and as we visited she explained how she had been baptized in Jesus name. She was one of those multitudes that had accepted Jesus name baptism and the infilling of the Holy Ghost but had not joined in to the classical groups. She was zealous and talked to everyone about baptism in Jesus name and had been instrumental in many officials being baptized and receiving the Holy Ghost. We bonded. Her husband worked with the Irby family and both her and her husband were heavily involved in politics. They had around them many powerful friends and Ruth Ann would use them to help me get things needed to do the work of God in Russia.

One day, I was very surprised to get a call at my house and on the other end of the phone was a sweet voice that said," Stanley?" And to my surprise I asked, "Is this Mrs. Fordice?" To which she responded, "yes". This caught me completely by surprise, as usually when even lower White House staff, or calls from persons at the governor's office, it was routine for a secretary to call ahead and say something such as, "Please, hold for the Governor." To call or be called and for such a person to answer directly was just shocking to me. It meant God had elevated me to a very special level. I greeted her again with surprise, so she asked," This is Stan, isn't it?" She then asked me if I could come over to the governor's mansion and I told her I was on my way. When I arrived, I was shown immediately into the office where I met Fred and Olga Lutsinko. The first lady asked me if I could help her with a little something. Can you imagine? It has been my great honor, given me by God, where he put me in such a position that Pres. Reagan, Bush, the governor of Mississippi, and the first lady, and other high officials would ask me to do them a favor. To this day, I laugh with joy that I was given these opportunities. Such powerful people, and yet God had placed me in a position where I could help them.

Pat's request was both spiritual and social. Olga had been one of the highest Soviet officials in the Ministry of Education. When the Soviet Union dissolved, this left Russia and the other republics in a quandary, as the basis of their society had been communism and atheism-now that was being dismissed. The question was, what would be the new basis for morals teaching in this country? A young person had been raised a communist all their life, grade after grade with classes on atheism and now the Ministry of Education no longer offered these classes. Olga had spoken to her bosses and said the United States had based much of their early teaching on the Bible, and it had been the underpinning of their morality. Now this was from a sociological position and was correct. Dismiss this and we leave our children to flounder. Because the Bible and all religious training had been stripped from the USSR they could see that what was needed was a reintroduction of the Bible and Biblical stories in the country. This is what I termed the "Reculturalization of Russia."

Mrs. Fordice Working with us to get Bibles and medical supplies to Russia.

N. A. Urshan and Dr. Olga Lutshanko.

On one hand, this fit within the confines of what I would consider the Bible and apostolic doctrine, because our doctrine grows out of the Scripture and therefore to present the Bible was, in my mind, to present apostolic doctrine. On the other hand, because it did not speak in a directly doctrinaire fashion that would produce the outward life of holiness and other aspects in the Word of God that called for real teaching; it was more of a socialization. This provided me with a great opportunity as I could pull together Presbyterians, Baptists, together with other religious groups, and have a significant place at the table for those apostolic pastors that wanted to join in this effort. Olga had put together a brilliant outreach that had started off with many evangelical groups called the Co-mission but had fizzled out. She had put together 27 Christian Resource Centers across the old Soviet Union. Each center at its facility provided by the country in which it resided, and a director whose salary was paid by the Ministry of Education, and in turn materials and Bibles for distribution were needed and funds were needed to purchase these and other workers. They also sponsored camps every summer, with special projects including artwork with Christian themes.

Pat Fordice was asking my help in organizing groups that would provide funding for these projects, and to help Fred and Olga. I explained that I was already overwhelmed with what I was doing, but possibly my wife would head up this project. I like this because it gave my wife prominence with the first lady and relationship with significant people. God laid on my heart to speak to one of the prominent families in Jackson, Mississippi, to get them involved-the person I contacted was Stuart Irby. He would often joke that when you want to catch big fish you've got to go where the big fish are, and Stan brought me on board because I know the big fish. This organized a second group, The Kindness Foundation which continues to work to this day in these projects. Over the years, they have done a tremendous job providing great blessing.

This meant that my wife and I were now working on three tracks. One, dealing directly with the apostolic churches in Russia seeking their promotion and seeing the truth go forward, the second track dealing with the distribution of Bibles, Christian literature, and camps, and the third track, was dealing sociologically with the overall reculturalization of Russia. In fact, this now had us working on a fourth track which was dealing with medical supplies and humanitarian relief that was purely humanitarian in its outreach, but also providing a building for the church in St. Petersburg. Now this final project was going to bring socialization to Mississippi and make the first lady incredibly popular. As a thank you, the city of St. Petersburg sent the palaces of St. Petersburg Exhibit to Jackson, Mississippi, and in addition about eight people were knighted by the grand order of St. John of Moscow via the Russian Orthodox Church. I was not knighted primarily because I was in their minds a heretic preacher. I was beginning to see this, then is the task that God had given me to minister to Russia. This is immense country covering 11-time zones and all its diversification that needed so much.

I will at this point, make a statement that will irritate many people, but it is a fact that we failed Russia and so many of the other countries that had been a part of the USSR. We did this as America and as the church. When it comes to America, we failed them in political terms as we changed administrations. Reagan and Bush had brought down the Soviet Union, and with it we had rushed in to provide food and monies that were needed desperately to salvage the lives of multitudes. The term "Bush legs" became synonymous with the chickens that we provided Russia for food that was primarily dark meat or hindquarters. When the administration changed, there was now little interest in working with Russia as that gave credit to those that had gone before, and thus millions of dollars were provided and sent to Russia without much accountability. On the one hand, it is hard for me to evaluate as the locals claim that most of the money was stolen by Yeltsin's daughter and shipped out of the country, on the other hand I did see significant investments in the infrastructure to help promote tourism. A blue panel of the Congress of the United States reports that most of the money was wasted, and you can read that for yourself. Despite the fact that there was a huge peace dividend, money appropriated for those regions was likely not used well. When it comes to the church in missions, there was the difficulty of no easy road to provide help. Had we paid attention and used our money wisely we might not have given rise to Vladimir Putin.

In 1993, Russia would receive a tremendous blessing in the person of Rev. William Turner, who would answer the call and become the first United Pentecostal Church International missionary to Russia. Now they had been doing work in this country before this time with Sister Irene in Moscow being a primary contact point. I had recommended her to Brother Urshan. For some time, she had helped both of us. The United Pentecostal Church would have a variety of A I M workers as missionaries across the old Soviet Union. In the early days, as a convenient measure to get in and stay in the country, they worked with ACE schools, but later began to develop churches. About the same time the nation was blessed with Mark Stumbo of the Assemblies of the Lord Jesus Christ who has been the most consistent and dedicated missionary on that field.

As missionaries began to come into the country I turned and intentionally tried to stay away, only taking say a brief visit in 1994 to St. Petersburg at the opening of the Bible school connected with the old Smorondinskis. Nevertheless, God placed tasks before me to get more and more involved. We remained active, with the Gov.'s wife, Pat Fordice, and the Kindness Foundation by serving on the board and giving advice. About this time, we became very active with the International Studies Program at Jackson State University. At first, we were involved with professors on the exchange program. We would visit with them, take them to dinner, bring them to church, take them to church conventions, travel in the United States, and in general treat them well. Because this was an ongoing project with new professors coming in each year or two, one would pass the word to the next one," Get in touch with Stan when you get there." Every year there would be new ones.

One year, there was a businesswoman that came on an exchange program, named Irene that stayed with us. Being very bright, we presented her with "Search for Truth" Bible study, which she studied diligently. Later, her and my son would become romantic, he would go on an exchange program to Russia and study there for a year, and there in Russia would marry her and give birth to our granddaughter Sophia, with our granddaughter Christina being brought into the marriage. This makes all that we have done in Russia both personal and family. Sadly, this marriage would come apart later, but we have wonderful grandchildren and great grandchildren. After studying, Irene was baptized in Jesus name, and at a church convention of the National Youth of the Assemblies of the Lord Jesus Christ she was filled with the Holy Ghost and spoke in tongues.

With most of the missionaries, functioning in large Capital Cities such as Moscow or St. Petersburg or Kiev, we now turn our attention out a way, going farther and farther out into the reaches of Russia. For the first 15 or 20 years, I avoided going to any other country but Russia feeling it needed the attention. There were easier places to work and headway could be made much faster in those other spots. I witnessed in those early years such a tremendous outpouring of the Holy Ghost with everyone hungry to hear the gospel. Americans were very popular and well-liked, and buildings would be filled just to hear someone such as myself preach.

Irene's city, called Brezhnev in the communist times, was an extremely nice city located on the Kama River and was the home of the Kamaz Truck Factory, the largest truck factory in the world. Before Irene's birth, her parents had moved to the city to build the glorious new communist society, and now all of that teaching was gone, and the city was called by its original name Naberezchny Chelny, which I always joked was an old Indian name as the meaning of the words are little boats or canoes by the river. The whole area was ripe with history as a major city in the area is Kazan, which was Genghis Khan's northern capital. The Republic of Tartarstan is the northernmost Islamic republic in the world. It is a Muslim state and has all that history. Surprisingly, there was a strong Jewish community there with their history as well, and I helped them and had many friends among the Jews. You can imagine the hardship that the Jews faced as they moved from communism to Islam. Most moved to Israel.

I watched in Tartarstan as the revival spread in those early days. I am a firm believer that the passage in Acts the 15th chapter referring to taking out from among the Gentiles a people for his name, refers to where God would place his name, and from the context leaders explaining that God poured out the Holy Ghost on the Gentiles. James is adding that the purpose of the pouring out of the Holy Ghost was to prepare a people to receive the message of his name. All across Russia multitudes were receiving the Holy Ghost and churches in the thousands were springing up overnight. In Chelny, God laid on the hearts of some very good Pentecostals in the Ukraine to come to this city and start a church. Now so as not to intentionally insult a particular individual, I will refer to a particular pastor as Pastor E. This pastor along with six men moved into this city and literally slept on kitchen floors to bring the Pentecostal message to this area. Now there were other works there that were more historic, but this was a fresh wave in which multitudes were coming in to the Spirit.

Irene contacted Pastor E and he indicated that he would like to meet with us and work together. When we first met, I was very careful to explain to him that we believed in baptism in Jesus name, and he told me this was no problem. In fact, he was very careful to say that this was what the Bible taught-to be baptized in Jesus name. I then began a working relationship with this man that was very productive as I was free to preach in his church and I was prepared to help him to move along in a better understanding of the Godhead and baptism. At first, I made a visit to this city and shared the gospel and preached in the church, and it was agreed that we would then hold a rather large conference in this city. In turn, I helped Pastor E come to the United States, visit and introduce him to various churches and ministers. His great desire was a church building that he was trying to finish. This was secondary to me as an understanding of the Scripture down in the heart was more important and would last if buildings were taken away. At this point, I worked with him only to raise money to put on a large conference, buy Bibles to give to the

296

pastors and people, and take doctrinal studies and translate them into Russian.

There were many that responded to this, what we called, "The Miracle of Tartarstan". I formed a friendship with John Hancock with whom I would make many trips in the future and he developed a great love for Russia and traveled all over it. Sandra Gonzalez went on this first trip and documented it and you can still find articles by her on the web to this day. Leaders of the Apostolic Assembly of the Faith in Christ Jesus, including Samuel Valverde, went on other trips, as did, David Hudson, with the United Pentecostal Church international. This was a great group with a powerful impact. This was a Conference on the Name, and we preached on the beauty and power of the name.

Again, we agreed to have another conference, and through the summer, money was raised with it being designated for this conference. At this conference, we rented a KGB campground, and hosted over 200 church leaders. This included food and housing, gave them all Bibles, 10,000 additional Bibles, and 2,000 doctrinal studies like, "Search for Christ". This doctrinal book became the official teaching book of the Assembly of God in that area. This was because they had nothing else to work with and we had at least provided them with some tools. Faith Barnaby was with us and did teaching as was Nelson Hight-and again John Hancock was with us in this group.

It was at the close of this conference we began to have trouble. Over the months that we had worked together,

Pastor E had become very excited about the Jesus name message and began to embrace it. He had signed papers with the Apostolic World Christian Fellowship and declared himself to be apostolic and that he believed in baptism in Jesus name, and was saying that he was trying to lead his congregation into this message. When Pastor E. returned to Russia, his church organization elevated him to the five-man executive board. I am convinced they did this because they did not want to lose him, and at this point he turned radically against the message. At this time many members of his congregation became interested in and convinced of the need to be baptized in Jesus name.

This was a spiritual matter, and not one being forced. These people believe that baptism in Jesus name was correct and felt it was something they needed to do for themselves. I did not want to cause division and wanted to keep the church in harmony and moving towards this doctrinal position, and so I went to the pastor directly both in person and in writing using a very good translator and told him these people wish to be baptized in Jesus name, and as their pastor I feel you should do that for the harmony of the congregation. My thinking was if he baptized in Jesus name and I continued to remain loyal to him and to the church, and assuming he was doing as he said in trying to move the congregation in this direction-it would help. His response was this is never to be discussed again.

John Hancock and S. E. Wachtstetter at the first Tartarstan conference

I left and returned with the express purpose of baptizing those that wish to be baptized in Jesus name. There were about 40 and we had a wonderful time with several praying through in receiving the Holy Ghost. My friend John Hancock was with me and Brother T began to take lead and would soon be Pastor T. At this time, I had the privilege of baptizing my granddaughter Christina in Jesus name.

It was decided that I would help them in starting a church together with John Hancock. This was exciting living in this present age where we have so much instantaneous technology where we can Skype one another and carry on conversations at a reasonable rate. I think it cost us ten cents a minute for a phone call, so we could talk for an hour for about six dollars. Brother T was a great translator, self-taught but a brilliant individual that had mastered the English language far better than most. He thought much more American than many I had met there. What we agreed to do was purchase a speakerphone and rent or buy an apartment which would later become a church. This apartment would be a meeting place on Sundays and midweek. At this place Pastor Hancock or I would call most times together and give a sermon or a Bible study. There were 40 that had been baptized and this was pretty much the attendance in each service. At the end we would speak individually with each person about their concerns and taking prayer request. Over a period of time, Brother T began to feel his call and gravitated into the position of pastor with our having to teaching less and less and him doing more and more.

It was decided that for his education and the financial needs of the congregation that we bring him to the United States and introduce him around to various churches. Over the 25 or 30 years that we have worked in Russia, we have worked in so many ways, but one aspect was bringing pastors and teachers from Russia to the United States on short fund-raising trips. One reason was for them to see churches here, to see how they operated, to see how they worshiped, and to bond with them in a brotherly way. Another learning process was what I termed my Bible school of the road. This was with either my wife or myself driving them around the nation with hours just sitting in a car which opened the door for them to begin to ask questions about different doctrinal views and in a nonconfrontational way to be able to sit and discuss what the Bible said about these teachings. There was also money, but we operated very lean compared with most missionary programs and were not doing what would be termed deputation work as churches would give as God laid on their hearts a one-time offering. I did not believe in investing in buildings because of the uncertainty of that region. With no private land ownership and with governments that routinely confiscate anything they want, I felt it unwise to put huge sums in the buildings. We always raised money for the purpose of conferences or teaching because I felt that would stay with them even if we were shut out later.

Those who received Bibles at the conference in Chelny wanted Stan to sign them. My daughter asked, "Did they know you didn't write that book Dad?"

Our attention then turned to helping Pastor T establish a congregation in Naberezchny, Chelny, in the Republic of Tartarstan. This was a great place to engage in evangelism and had it all, communism, Islam, old Soviet mentality, and now freedom. Many reached out to us here, even the Jewish community with whom I would fellowship and spoke on many occasions. We had been well received by various church groups and had done much to help them. There were other present works such as Pastor Sten, and old

Urshanites. I received a letter from Pastor Sten many years later. It said he wanted me to know that our work in Tartarstan was not in vain and the church was still going and the help we had given him in starting a printing business had helped many and was still helping.

Pastor Sten in Tartarstan, Russia.

On the mission field, you fight great battles and I will share with you one of the most horrible of my life. Pastor T and others were in the country raising money for the work back in Russia and were being escorted around by my wife Helen while I was working for the Governor of Mississippi. I was sitting in my lounge chair one Saturday morning and it was raining, a rather sleepy time, when the phone rang. My daughter, Mary Alice, informed me that she and my son-in-law, Greg Harris, along with my 7-week-old grand-daughter Alice were on their way to help my niece who had called them informing of the fact that she had gone into the median during the rain storm. With Deanna being new to the area, Mary and Greg decided to go and try and help her and at the very least be there to comfort her while a tow truck came to help. I told them to keep me posted. In about 30 minutes I received another phone call. Someone anonymously said to me," You'd better get out to the exit on the west side of town." A trusted friend, Dan Frakes, went with me, and there we found a horrific automobile accident with an 18-wheeler, and my daughter standing in the rain holding my granddaughter Alice. Alice had that grey pallor to her that I had seen in others at their death, her scalp was bleeding, and looked much like hamburger. Mary was crying, and Alice seemed lifeless and without breath. The emergency people were in the process of placing her in the ambulance and they said to my daughter that she could not go in the ambulance, I quickly laid hands on her and prayed for her and for Mary. My daughter, Mary Alice, said to them, "I'm going with her", and they said, "you cannot". She said," I am going with her!" They finally relented and told her she could ride up front with the driver. As they drove Mary asked if Alice would be all right, it seemed the driver was doing her best to hold back tears. Mary began to pray "God heal my baby but if you must take her I will still always love you and work for you. About that time, Alice started crying and the driver said, "that's a very good sign".

What had happened was as Greg, Mary, little Alice and Deanna were waiting beside the road for the tow truck to come to get my nieces' car pulled out of the ditch, a semi-truck began to slide down the road sideways and ran into the back of Greg's car. Greg had some cracked vertebrae and a ruptured disk in his back which required surgery, Deanna had damage to her spleen, and Mary had a damaged rotator cuff and hip (which she suffers from today) while my little 7-week old granddaughter had a fractured skull.

My Daughter, Mary Alice Harris, visiting the wrecked car after she got out of the hospital.

Sadly, that was not the end of that week, when I got home there was an email from Russia. It was pastor T's wife writing to say their baby had an accident in his stroller and had died! I immediately called Helen and told her and asked her to let Pastor T know. The next day I cancelled the remainder of their schedule and Helen rushed Pastor T to Washington, D. C. to catch a flight back to Russia!

Over a prolonged period of time, this put Pastor T and his wife in a downward spiral that ended with him out of the church, them divorced, and the church destroyed. I do not judge, but I pray for them both individually and still as a family.

The fact that it happened at the same time makes it clear that the devil was trying to stop the work we were all doing in Russia.

God continued to open doors for me and I ministered in Volgograd, formerly Stalingrad, and this included two or three trips and involved the neighboring community of Volzhsky, where my son had studied. I had the privilege of teaching some classes in the college there and made friends with a Pastor S. I held two or three conferences in that region including a very special one on Christian education inviting churches from as far as Bashkiria to attend with conference speakers Peggy Clifford, of Little Rock Arkansas, and Barbara Strickland who were both great educators, not just in church work, but also in public education, along with myself, having graduated the school of education at the University of Idaho. These ladies put on such a phenomenal teaching session and I had the privilege of traveling with them. We were in Moscow, as well as, Volgograd. The teaching was outstanding. It was a real bridge maker presenting great truth and doctrine. They made puppets, presented various activities and games for children and youth, and even had a clown suit. This clown was incredibly popular, and the Russian girl that wore it said it had always been her dream to do something like this. It was a wonderful time of teaching and we were able to bless many that had come into the conference.

About this time, Pastor E was contacted by the Republic of Bashkiria in the Russian federation and asked to meet me. I met with him and his family and with about seven pastors in that region. I made two trips there, one being with Peter Rowe and I was able to raise funds to purchase this wonderful log cabin church out in the far reaches of European Russia close to the Ural Mountains. This was one of my happiest moments, as this was not the great cities of St. Petersburg or Moscow, it was not the masses of humanity, this was the simple countryside. I had not helped to build some great edifice or magnificent building but a simple, humble log cabin where the gospel would be preached in the rural areas.

My ministry was different than many others doing missions work. They set up shop and go to work in one location and begin to build around them and this is desperately needed, but it is not what God called me to do. From my first entry, I felt the door would close one day and things may go back to the old ways (of this I hope I am wrong.) Pastors were interested in buildings, but I was interested in souls and I wanted to plant as much seed as I could possibly plant in various areas knowing that the Holy Ghost could raise up a harvest. I preached across the country all the way to the Far East. I took advantage of anyone that wanted to go to Russia to connect with them to stretch the funds that I had as I operated on a shoestring. I suppose all the monies that I spent over 30 years would not equal the money that is allocated for most missionaries for one year. I did raise large sums of medical supplies for the city of St. Petersburg, monies for Bibles and meetings in general, monies for buildings, and monies for ministries there which would've amounted to quite a bit of money, but for myself I spent very little. I found it miraculous that in my first four trips I flew free and I flew business class. This was a miracle of God and I felt a sign of his approval. It was free because airlines or tour groups would sponsor me in the hope that later they would reap some benefit. Two or more trips were because I was taking a group large enough that my airline ticket was covered. One time when I was taking a group, I had negotiated a very low-fare of about $700 round-trip on Delta Airlines and when I got to New York I was confused because I was arriving late, but my friend David Hudson had been approached by the airline that they needed the space and they provided him with a $1,000 airline credit for each person on the trip. When we got to Amsterdam our whole group was bumped again, and I argued that they each deserve another thousand dollars' credit which took some fighting but after several months they gave each person $1,000, and myself $2,000 because I was the tour host, and my wife and myself an upgrade pass to business class. It seemed I had God's approval on what I was doing and therefore I could spend most of my time raising money to help them and not myself.

On one occasion, Bishop Peter Rowe accompanied myself and my son-in-law, Greg Harris across much of Russia on the trans-Siberian Railway. Bishop Rowe was so gracious and kind to us and helped in so many ways. I can never tell him how thankful I was for all that he did as he stood there and ministered at a drug rehabilitation center out in the most desolate of areas on a farm in which these folks who had given their lives to Christ were trying to rehabilitate and wanted to be shut off from any temptation. He ministered and preached to thousands at Perm.

The work that was done across the old Soviet Union was a teamwork effort in which I involved family and friends. One must understand that my wife, Helen, should receive every bit as much credit as I for the work that was done over these last 30 years. Not only did she support me and encourage me to but at times she climbed in the van and took nationals from those countries around from church to church raising money, she scheduled me to speak out, she organized the Kindness Foundation, and in general when it was necessary preached across Russia herself. My son, Jon, took groups around the nation to help raise funds, and he went and lived in Russia for a year. My daughter, Mary, worked tirelessly and went to Russia with me on various occasions. If I started to list all the friends that went, and gave money, and hosted people from that part of the world I would leave someone out and that would be unfair. There is an old saying," success has 1,000 fathers."

S.E. Wachtstetter, Pastor Kasheev (Smorodons Grandson) from Kazan and John Hancock.

Until about six years ago, I had focused entirely on Russia and not ventured out because I felt it was underrepresented and much more difficult to deal with as a whole. There were so many others working in the other republics that were far more open than Russia, but two things happened that changed my thinking, and that was: 1. Putin started taking the country backwards into the old mentality, and 2. Others began to reach out and plead with me to come there.

When I say that Putin began to take the nation backwards, I mean there became a strong appearance that there would be a revitalization of something such as the old Soviet Union; and, therefore, something needed to be done to prepare for what I called a fallback position. If Russia was going to be reached with the gospel in the future we needed a spot where even if we were shut out of the country of Russia, pastors from there could come receive teaching and help and be sent back. Ukraine seemed the best spot for this to take place. They were an independent nation and, yet they had had long years with interaction between themselves and the Russians. Ukraine is a word that means "the border." It has a long history of serving as a buffer between so many warring factions such as, Germany, Poland, and Russia, as well as others. This means that there are areas in the Ukraine that are very Russian, and this would be similar to the southern parts of Texas and California on the Mexican border in which those areas might appear almost Mexican, but in fact are the United States. If you go to the western side of the Ukraine it will seem like Germany with many communities speaking German and culturally German. Slightly to the North and to the West you will find large Polish communities. This was the historic purpose of the Ukraine-to provide this buffer area. This meant the Ukraine would serve as a natural fallback position because of the interaction with the different countries. It would be hard for me to have seen at the time the tremendous Russian hostility that was going to develop towards a Ukraine that would not fly the Russian flag and be subservient.

Others began to reach out to me such as David Fuller and Sonny Cathy of the Apostolic World Christian Fellowship. Bishop Fuller called me and said that on the Internet he had received a contact from a pastor in the Ukraine that wanted truth on the apostolic doctrine, and that he was going to make a trip to go teach a leadership conference in Izmial, Ukraine and would I go with him. Now this offered me the fact-finding opportunity that I wanted as without any obligation I would be able to simply go and see what was there. Everything was arranged, and Bishop Fuller was going to Minister in England and fly to the Ukraine where I would meet him, but on his flight, he had a heart episode and he felt it best that he go back home. This meant I was teaching the leadership conference. I found here a pastor that loved the word of God and a large group of believers that were very sweet and wonderful. You cannot imagine how much they went out of their way to accommodate me.

Now they were having a real camp meeting on the banks of the Danube River, and they were staying in pup tents and sleeping on the ground. The meals were cooked over an open fire much like the Chuck wagon, and the toilet is simply a hole in the ground.

When they saw me at my size and my delicacies they arranged a bed be brought out to the site and erected a special toilet with a chair that did not have a seat in it but would serve the purpose. But even at that, when the pastor of a Christian Evangelical church in a small town close to their campsite heard I was there he insisted I be moved into his house and sleep in his bed. I begged him to not do this, but it was explained to me it would have been an insult to not accept it. They were so hospitable, and it was a wonderful time of rest and spiritual blessing. I taught twice a day and it reached into the evening. I felt the anointing of God as His Word went forth. This bonded us, and I was accepted as overseer or mentor.

I would return to the city many times, and the next occasion was Christmas. I learned something over my years in Russia as the fact that their Christmas is on January 7. I started the project with having a banquet for widows and a separate great dinner for the orphans. I dressed up as Santa

Claus and distributed gifts to the children and had just a wonderful time. Because of the difference in timing between their Christmas and ours, I was able to buy cookies, candies, and goodies at an extremely reduced rate 75% off and sometimes as high as 90% off. This was so much fun. I can remember staying up with the pastor and his wife filling bags with various goodies both for the orphans and for the children and the church.

Now for an orphan there is perhaps no lonelier day of the year than Christmas. It is a reminder that he has no family and that he is alone. The staff in the orphanage will use their seniority to get the day off to be able to be home with their families and thus Christmas can be a rather bleak time for an orphan. But by God's grace we were able to turn this around. People had given, and we were able to put on a large fashionable banquet in an elegant place for the widows and the church. As Ukrainians they sang, danced, celebrated and enjoyed the occasion. I had joy in seeing their joy. For the orphans, we planned a great banquet. It was agreed to get several chickens and have one for each table with all the trimmings and pastries. They put on a presentation for me telling me how much they loved what was happening. They had practiced for weeks. Now the staff were each given a Christmas card, a Christmas hat, and in their card, each got cash, which was not very much by our standards but was over a week's wages for them. When the word was out all the staff in the orphanage used their seniority, not to bump to get the day off, but to be able to be there for this Christmas event. The newspaper came out, the television station came out, and there was good media for the church. And we did all of this, the widows, the orphans, candies and gifts for the children that the church, and the staff for all under $2,000. Thank you, Jesus! What is even better is the church there has maintained this themselves now every year. On occasion, we help them but even if we don't they do it on their own.

When I came to the city it hit me just how much had occurred and that was about 20 years at that time. There was this massive change, even in the looks of the country. What had been gray and dark when I arrived in 1990, now flowers bloomed, bright colors and bright lights and it was just very pleasant. When I first arrived, Bibles were still outlawed, and there were few if any church buildings, but now large congregations exist with more than one in each city, and beautiful buildings. In the city, there were six good churches that were Jesus name. I could not help but reflect what a massive revival had quietly taken place across the old Soviet Union. It was about this time that I began to reflect on that so often you see a person and the church from a life of alcoholism or drug addiction and watched the miraculous change in their life to the point that years later people might think they've been raised in the church all of their lives and never knew much outside of it. I realized that it was just as easy for God to do that for a nation as it was a person.

I continue to do this work in missions even though it is more taxing as I get older. God blessed me in my old age and gave me a situation that is comfortable, but still permits travel from time to time. I was helping this pastor from Ukraine to raise money for his church, as we had on various occasions; I would take them around from church to church and they would give their presentation and we would try to raise money this way. They needed $20,000 to finish their building. They were in desperate straits, as it was turning fall and would soon be winter and they had no heat for their building, nor were they able to move inside. During their building program, they had been worshiping outdoors in a tent like structure. We started preaching around visiting churches and churches gave quite liberally. We had reached a point where over that time we had raised about $11,000, but $5,000 had been needed to cover their airfare and some travel expenses here in the United States. There were two more weeks left and we were only up about $6,000 and it appeared that there was little hope. It is always in these moments that God works the greatest miracles. We felt impressed to go to Texas. We began to preach in churches connected with a friend of ours named Pastor Trevino. These were Spanish-speaking churches and while we had had the trouble of translating from Russian to English, on at least one occasion we had the humorous situation of them speaking in Russian and a person translating into English so that the Spanish translator not knowing Russian but knowing English good then translated into Spanish. These were nice churches with people that were willing to give the best they could, but the offerings were way smaller than we had previously received. We began to feel we had missed the will of God, and yet there was this nagging feeling we had been called here.

During this time, we were with our friend, Pastor Trevino, and he asked me if I knew Jack Liford, and I told him, of course, we had been children together in the same city, and in the same church, Calvary Tabernacle, and we had known each other well, but I had not seen him for 50 years. Now think of that, someone you had not visited with for 50 years, except perhaps to have been in some large assemblage together, and here we were together in Texas.

Pastor Trevino had been building a church, and was still in the process, and he had a building inspector that either hated Hispanics, or Apostolics, or both. It seemed this inspector had gone well out of his way to make life difficult for Pastor Trevino. Finally, in desperation, pastor went to deep prayer and pleaded with God to remove that building inspector, and within three days he was gone. The city of Hillsboro, Texas, contracted with Jack Liford to come in as the new inspector. The first day the two men met, Jack said, "I see your sign out front says Apostolic, are you Apostolic?" The pastor thought to himself, not again, but boldly said," Yes, I am from the top of my head to the bottom of my feet." Jack said," So am I." Jack of course did his job, but now in a friendly manner and the two visited with each other from time to time, and when he told Jack that Stan would be with him in service, Jack said I would like to see my old friend. It was agreed we would have lunch together.

While we were at lunch eating, Jack asked me, what I was doing there? The Ukrainian pastors were with me, and I explained we were raising funds to be able to finish their building to get the congregation in and out of the cold. At this point, he started explaining to me about this church in Arlington, Texas, it was what Paul Mooney might say was on the periphery of Pentecost, but to me was the very heart of that movement. It was not strong on organization, but neither was it opposed to any of the Apostolic denominations. It believed all the rather, traditional aspects of the Oneness Pentecostal doctrines, including holiness, but was not culturally attuned. To me it was the very center of the apostolic movement, and I was delighted when they invited me to be their pastor.

Here I met Mike Robertson he was a great financial blessing to the work in the Ukraine. We are friends and have traveled together. The church here has provided for my needs making the raising of funds for me to live far less demanding and has helped in many projects and travel, so I travel and take missions as my health permits. This has provided me the opportunity for my ministry to go in a new direction and being able to write. I now have the time and resources to tell all God has done and it is marvelous in our sight.

Stanley and Helen Wachtstetter.

Going to a State Dinner at the White House for President Diouf of Senegal. September 11, 1991. We stayed with our friends from MS. who was then the Assistant Secretary of Labor under President Bush. When they found out we were invited to the dinner they invited us to stay with them. Col. Tom Collins III and his wife Donny were a remarkable couple.

Old Russian Church

# Chapter Seven

## Prophecy

## Of

## Gog and Magog

As I write the word Magog it brings to mind, for most Americans, an extremely negative connotation. That should not be the case, as Magog is a son of Japheth, and a grandson of Noah. Very few references are made to Magog in the Bible. It is surprising how few times the word Magog appears in the Bible. In addition, prophecy is often quite unclear. Nevertheless, I do not wish to avoid this subject.

The Cold War developed a mental hostility between those of us in the West and those in the Old Soviet Union, or what we generally called Russia. When the iron curtain came down we had great hope for the immediate future of Russia. The transition was not easy, and it went into an economic freefall. The number of rubles that it would take to buy a car in 1991 when I first visited the country would buy a bottle of water when I came back in 1994. Putin stepped in and stabilized the ruble. It had fallen so bad it was about 30,000 to the dollar. He simply removed the thousand marks, making it 30 rubles to the dollar and caused it to hold in place. This caused the economy to surge, and there was democracy, and freedom of worship. He was putting good policies in place that was putting

Russia on the world stage. At some point he made a turn and started going backwards, dismissing elections of governors, invading Ukraine, picking a fight with the United States, placing heavy restrictions on churches of the evangelical faith or any faith other than Russian Orthodox.

Russia has been hurt badly over the last few years with people not trusting its economy and its ruble cut in half. This has caused economic hardship on the country and greatly restricted it. I keep hoping for the best and hoping for what they term - a reset. This does not seem likely, but we can always hope for the very best for this nation.

When it comes to prophecy, the key scripture for this very moment is Matthew 24:14, "and this gospel of the kingdom shall be preached in all the world for a witness unto all nations; and then shall the end come." The message to the church for this hour is to love Magog with the same love that Paul wrote of in the book of Colossians, the same love of John 3:16, to preach THIS of the kingdom to Magog. Here is the most important Prophetic message of this moment. It was prophesied by Jesus and we are in that hour.

There are a couple of things that I wish to share in reference to prophecy that I had not heard preached before nor have I heard comment. I want to emphasize that the Russian people in general are very sweet by nature, and many would give you the shirt off their back. If they are your friend, they are a true friend.

Magog will be referred to only three times in Bible prophecy, twice in Ezekiel, and once in Revelations. Ezekiel is careful to say very little against Magog. In the scripture it draws a clear distinction between Gog and Magog. Gog is the Chief Prince while Magog is the country or the people. God does not set his face against Magog anywhere in the Ezekiel text. Three times the prophet is commanded to speak to Gog, and twice is commanded to set his face against him. This threefold witness is significant, but I have never heard, in all my years in the church, a preacher draw a distinction between Gog and Magog. This is a very important distinction, and not just a distinction but a separation, and would be well known by the people living there and any one that is clearly studied history. Over the millenniums there has been a great distinction between the peoples of that land and the governance. First, the Tartars ruled, taxed and brutalized the people. There was little to no relationship between the government and the people. Next, came the Rus as conquerors and they ruled over the people there. This evolved into the Czars and serfdom slavery. Afterwards, came the communist. Seldom has Magog any say in her policies.

After Korea and Vietnam, the death of our children and the suffering of so many here in America it is easy to be bitter towards the land of Russia. I want to point out that no one has suffered at the hands of the government of Russia more than the Russian people. The death toll in the gulags was in the scores of millions, and the suffering was constant and ongoing. No one suffered more from Russia then Russians.

For some there is a debate if Magog is really Russia. There are so many ways to establish this fact. There is the reference to it being the Kingdom of the North, and if you go north from Jerusalem you will pass through Moscow. Some writers have rather far-fetched reasoning. While it is generally held by the Encyclopedia Judaic that Magog goes north of the Black Sea, others push this point. Queen Christina, Queen of Sweden had documents written giving a lineage back to Magog claiming this ancient as the founder of that nobility with her as the 42nd ruler. While this is all speculation when you study burial practice and cultures between Scythians and Norse there is great similarities. Should the family of Magog have gone so far north they would then re-enter their homeland as the Rus?

Magog is also the Kingdom of the East. Russia is divided by the Ural Mountains; all East is Asia everything West is Europe. Magog is of lesser importance and is not addressed directly. Everyone would accept the fact that Russia is the land of the Scythians, and it is clear that Josephus states that the Jews called them Magog. This is important because Ezekiel would have understood Magog to be Russia.

Of greater clarity is Gog, which is termed the Chief Prince. This is very interesting, a prince, not a King. Why a prince? Why the Chief Prince? This is a title I have only heard of among the Rus. When the Rus invaded the lands of Ukraine, Belarus and Russia they established principalities, and built kremlins (or forts/castles). They would dominate their region, gather taxes and dominate their areas under permission of the Tartars. In fact, each spring each prince would bring taxes to the Tartars and whoever brought the most was permitted to wear a crown and was declared the Chief Prince or the Prince of Princes among the Rus. Rurick was the first ruler and he came in and unified the Rus, but on his death the Rus were divided with each son a "prince". This is a very interesting title.

Now let us consider the title "Chief Prince of Mesheck and Tubal." Remember in the old Hebrew there were no vowels, these are added for convenience but not always accurate. A very possible identification is the ancient city of Tobol or Tobolsk on the river of the same name. Both would be TBL with vows added accordingly. This ancient city was the early center of power for Siberia. Now in the same manner Mesheck easily becomes Moshock or Moscov (the Jews come closer to this in their translation). We say Moscow, but Russians say Moscov. These names are so close as to be clear. Thus, the title Chief Prince of Moscow and Tobol or the leader of Russia and Siberia, and as such the Ruler of the North and the East.

Some have tried to take the word Chief in Hebrew which is Rosh to refer to Russia and the Rus. I do not. Certainly, it is close sounding. Rosh means first, the head, thus Rosh Hashanah. Some have argued it was so far north and thus the head or the first, but this is weak. Since we don't know the origin of Rus it is difficult to say there is or is not a linage. There may be some Japhetic theoretical language that links them?

There will be an army that follows this maniac Gog to their death on the battle fields of Israel. This is not the whole of the Russian people. This prophecy is important because it speaks of God's love. He addresses this leader directly knowing he is wicked enough he will read it, hear it, and see it and yet dismiss it. As far as Russian Pentecostals are concerned most are pacifists with a long history of rejecting such leaders.

There are, also, two passages in Daniel I find of great interest that I have never heard commented. Daniel 11:30, "The ships of Chittim shall come against him: therefore, he shall be grieved, and return, and have indignation against the holy covenant: so, shall he do; he shall even return, and have intelligence with them that forsake the holy covenant."

Who are these ships? One interpretation is they are from the West. I like to think they are the United States Navy. At any rate the prophecy seems clear, the anti-Christ will be in motion and will start down but be turned back. Interesting. He will do intelligence work. He is determined to his destruction. I don't remember ever hearing that the Antichrist would be turned back. He will do intelligence work, this is such a modern term, or at least I think it's such. Imagine, spying of the land and working with people that were in a strategic war.

Another passage I find of extreme interest, Daniel number 11: 44-45," but tidings out of the east and out of the north shall trouble him: therefore, he shall go forth with great fury to destroy, and utterly to take away many. And he shall plant his tabernacles of his palace between the seas in the glorious holy mountain, yet he shall come to his end, and none shall help him." And here is a passage I have never heard emphasized which I feel offers a real positive for the people of Russia. Drawing from the Ezekiel passage and assuming Gog will be leading an army of Russia and her allies. He will set up his command post at Meggido or between there and the Mediterranean Sea and using previous interpretation of scriptures and we conclude the north and the east to be Russia and Siberia, and he will hear of trouble there. What is the trouble? We don't know. Based on the fact, and none shall come to help, it appears that the Russian people or Magog will turn against Gog. He likely will be sending for reinforcements, but these people have had enough of him.

There is another great battle at the end of the world, the battle of Gog and Magog. However, because this involves every nation of the world and because this is the spot of the origin of the spread of men this is neither a positive nor a negative on any nation or people.

When starting from the creation, I tried to pass through every age, from the creation of man in the garden, through the flood, to the resettlement of the world, the rise of the Scythians, the civilized Roman world, through the age of the Czar, and the Pentecostal revival, to the present, and into Biblical prophecy. We have ridden horses with the Scythians, observed their burial practices, speculated their outcome, visited Mykop, learned of revivals, learned of apostolic teaching-ancient and modern-in this region. I hope I have built a bridge of understanding and perhaps respect.

# Epilogue

In getting this book together the cover had been a problem. While many ideas were floated one came to mind that we use a map of Russia and show the many men that God used to reach Russia with the Gospel. I wanted to list these men in tribute to the great work that was being done. As I began listing them I was so impressed with the love and sacrifice shown. I wanted to include them in the epilogue if it didn't make the cover because of its significance. Names like Shatrov that recur over and over. The Russian church in the Spirit of the Apostles have records of the pastors that were killed in prison and the name Shatrov is one of them. It gives me great pleasure to include the Grandson of Somordon, Nikolai Kasheev, as one of the modern-day pastors as well as many Shatrovs.

**Wherefore seeing we also are compassed about with so great a cloud of witnesses. Hebrews 12:1**

# RUSSIA

Noah, Japheth, Apostle Andrew, A.D. Urshan, Alexander I. Ivanov, Goryachin, Averkien

Nikolai P Smorodin, Fortuna, Jan Sikora,

V. Sukhorukov, G. Blinov, K. Shatrov, Rudko

A. Smirnov, V. Kalegin, N. Shishkov, R. Nolte,

Q. Pitke, Al Bordukov, S. Makarov, Ya Arbuzov,

M. Averkiev, P. N. Koloskov, Gramocicn,

N. A. Urshan, Harry Scism, Norman Rutzen,

Dmitry Shatrov Sr. Stanley E. Wachtstetter,

Victor Shatrov, Mark Stumbo, William Turner,

Samuel Smith, Leonid Kissel, Alexander Shatrov,

Peter Shatrov, Robert Kaev, Alexander Krudin,

Norman Yadon, Audrey Shatrov,

Nikola Kasheev, Dmitry Shatrov Jr,

Robert McFarland, Wlliam Turner,

John Hancock, Pastor Sten, Peter Rowe

Wachtstetter Foundation

P. O. Box 1238

Batesville, MS 38606

Made in the USA
Middletown, DE
18 March 2022